FORD MADOX FORD
A REAPPRAISAL

Edited by
Robert Hampson
and
Tony Davenport

Amsterdam - New York, NY 2002

The Ford Madox Ford Society

The publication of this volume of International Ford Madox Ford Studies was made possible thanks to the generous support of the Joseph Conrad Society (UK) and the Juliet McLauchlan Bequest.

Cover illustration: Ford Madox Ford at the Bungalow, Winchelsea, c. 1903. Reproduced by kind permission of the Hon. Oliver Soskice. Ford c.1915, pen and ink drawing, © Alfred Cohen, 2000

The paper on which this book is printed meets the requirements of "ISO 9706:1994, Information and documentation - Paper for documents - Requirements for permanence".

ISBN: 90-420-0953-5 (bound)
©Editions Rodopi B.V., Amsterdam - New York, NY 2002
Printed in The Netherlands

FORD MADOX FORD

A REAPPRAISAL

International
Ford Madox Ford
Studies
Volume 1

General Editor
Max Saunders, King's College Londen

For information about the Ford Madox Ford Society,
please see the website at:
www.rialto.com/fordmadoxford_society

or contact:
max.saunders@kcl.ac.uk
or
Dr Sara Haslam s.j.haslam@open.ac.uk
Department of Literature, Open University,
Walton Hall, Milton Keynes, MK7 6AA, UK

Guidelines for contributors to IFMFS, including a full list of
abbreviations of Ford's titles and related works, can be found on
the website. Abbreviations used in this volume are listed on pp.
187-91.

CONTENTS

GENERAL EDITOR'S PREFACE

Max Saunders

Ford Madox Ford has as often been a subject of controversy as a candidate for literary canonization. He was, nonetheless, a major presence in early twentieth-century literature, and he has remained a significant figure in the history of modern English and American literature for over a century now. Throughout that time he has been written about – not just by critics, but often by leading novelists and poets, such as Graham Greene, Robert Lowell, William Carlos Williams, Gore Vidal, A. S. Byatt, and Julian Barnes. His two acknowledged masterpieces have remained in print since the 1940s. *The Good Soldier* now regularly figures in studies of Modernism and on its syllabuses. *Parade's End* has been increasingly recognized as comparably important. It was described by Malcolm Bradbury as 'a central Modernist novel of the 1920s, in which it is exemplary'; by Anthony Burgess as 'the finest novel about the First World War'; and by Samuel Hynes as 'the greatest war novel ever written by an Englishman'.

During the last decade or so, there has been a striking resurgence of interest in Ford and in the multifarious aspects of his work. As befits such an international and internationalist phenomenon as Ford himself, this critical attention has been markedly international, manifesting itself not only in the United Kingdom and the U. S. A., but in Continental Europe and beyond. Many of his works have not only been republished in their original language, but also translated into more than a dozen others.

The founding of the International Ford Madox Ford Studies series reflects this increasing interest in Ford's writing and the wider understanding of his role in literary history. Each volume will normally be based upon a particular theme or issue. Each will relate aspects of Ford's work, life, and contacts, to broader concerns of his time.

PREFACE

The spirit of this first volume is also the spirit in which the series has been established: to reappraise Ford for the twenty-first century; to explore his range and richness; to chart his relations with other writers and artists, whether his precursors, contemporaries, or later readers.

The note of the volume is a celebration of Ford's diversity. As the editors argue, his versatility comes to the fore as he moves between satire, fantasy, psychological fiction, poetry, and criticism (whether of literature, art or culture). The diversity and intelligence of his engagement with the art and thought of his age also comes across strongly. There is fresh work on his relation to figures whose names are familiar in Ford studies: the Pre-Raphaelites, Henry James, Ezra Pound, Sigmund Freud. And the range is extended to include less familiar, but also significant negotiations with writers such as Mark Twain, H. G. Wells, Marcel Proust, Richard Aldington, Wyndham Lewis, and T. S. Eliot.

Future volumes are planned which will focus on Ford's best-known work, and on his writings on culture. This first volume launches the process of reappraisal with studies of some of the best of his poetry, writings on art, and less well-known fiction: *A Call, The Simple Life Limited, The Marsden Case,* and *The Rash Act.*

The series is published in association with the Ford Madox Ford Society. Forthcoming and projected volumes will be announced on the Society's web site, together with details of whom to contact with suggestions about future volumes or contributions. The address is: **www.rialto.com/fordmadoxford_society**

INTRODUCTION

Tony Davenport and Robert Hampson

In 1946, Granville Hicks included *The Good Soldier* in an article entitled 'My Favorite Forgotten Books'.[1] In retrospect, however, Hicks's article takes its place as part of a post World War II rediscovery of Ford.[2] In that same year Penguin reprinted *The Good Soldier*, and, two years later, added *Some Do Not ...* , *No More Parades*, *A Man Could Stand Up* – and *Last Post* to their list. In America, 1948 saw a Ford Madox Ford symposium in the *Princeton University Library Chronicle*.[3] This included what were to be two very influential articles: Mark Schorer's 'The Good Novelist in *The Good Soldier*' and Robie Macaulay's 'The Good Ford'. 'The Good Ford' was subsequently reprinted in the *Kenyon Review* and in John Crowe Ransom's *The Kenyon Critics*, and, when *Parade's End*, the tetralogy as a single volume, was published in America in 1950, a revised portion of Macaulay's article was used for the Introduction.[4] Similarly, when *The Good Soldier* was reprinted in America the following year, Schorer's article became the Preface.

In this sequence of events, we see not just the rediscovery of Ford, however, but also the institutionalisation of a particular version of Ford, which emphasises *The Good Soldier* and *Parade's End* to the exclusion of almost all Ford's other works. Kenneth Young's 1956 pamphlet on Ford did add *The Fifth Queen* to *The Good Soldier* and *Parade's End*, and the 1961 *Concise Cambridge History of English Literature* found room to praise Ford's reminiscences (as well as mentioning *The Good Soldier* and *Parade's End*).[5] However, even a comparatively recent work like Robert Green's *Ford Madox Ford: Prose and Politics* concentrates on *The Fifth Queen, The Good Soldier* and *Parade's End* and offers only a brief chapter on what it calls 'the later fiction'.[6] Similarly, Ann Barr Snitow's excellent study, *Ford Madox Ford and the Voice of Uncertainty*, which does devote space to works such as *The Benefactor, An English Girl, A Call, The Simple Life Limited* and *The*

New Humpty-Dumpty treats them, in effect, largely as apprentice work leading up to the writing of *The Good Soldier* and *Parade's End*; and she dismisses the later novels (without further consideration) as 'frozen exercises in Edwardian sensibility'.[7] The rediscovery of Ford has taken place within clearly marked limits.

Ford's success as an editor has also tended to work against him. There has been a critical tendency to reduce Ford to the role of adjunct to and enabler of other authors' careers: D. H. Lawrence and Wyndham Lewis are obvious examples. Ford has also tended to be eclipsed by his one-time collaborator, Joseph Conrad, who was also critically re-discovered in the 1950s. R. L. Mégroz, in *Joseph Conrad's Mind and Method* (1931), sets the tone with his presentation of the collaboration: Ford 'could teach little about writing to the author of *Almayer* and *The Nigger of the 'Narcissus'*.[8] Jocelyn Baines, in *Joseph Conrad: A Critical Biography*, similarly observes that 'Conrad was a writer of considerable standing and achievement' at the time of the collaboration, whereas Ford 'had done little more than show brilliant promise'.[9] More damning, however, is the tone of Baines's references to Ford's 'extraordinarily garbled' stories and 'wildly inaccurate statements'.[10] It is only comparatively recently that Ford's role in the collaboration has had justice done to it and the accuracy of his statements has been re-assessed. As the editors of the *Oxford Reader's Companion to Conrad* observe: 'Allusions to Ford's notorious "unreliability" have been common in Conrad scholarship for many years, together with charges that Ford exaggerated his own importance to Conrad, but the surviving documentary evidence has validated many of Ford's claims'.[11] Ford's writing of memoirs and reminiscences has, on this evidence, been very damaging to his subsequent reputation. He has been described as 'an extremely unreliable and inventive recorder, a small-beer Frank Harris'.[12] Above all, however, it is Ford's reputation as a poet that has suffered the greatest slump. Though Pound could describe him in 1913 as 'the best lyrist in England', Ford the poet almost disappeared in the second half of the twentieth century, largely because, after the *Collected Poems* of 1936 (which was, in any case, never published in

Britain) few of his poems were in print. There was the slim *Selected Poems: Ford Madox Ford* of 1971 (also published in America); a more substantial *Selected Poems* did not become available until 1997.[13]

Despite all this, there has been a slow revival of interest in Ford in recent years, originally stemming more from Ford's involvement in major literary movements and with other major literary figures than from his own neglected writings. It has also had a strongly biographical basis. Arthur Mizener and Alan Judd, in their different ways, take Ford's life, works and complexity of relationships as the country whose geography they are exploring and mapping.[14] Ford's fiction and other imaginative writings, though often interestingly discussed, are inevitably looked at within biographical contexts. Ford's reputation does, however, finally seem to be on the turn, and the turning-point is marked by another, more recent biography: Max Saunders's monu- mental two-volume critical biography.[15] From the outset, Saunders refuses to use Ford's writings merely 'to support an account of his life' (I, 9). Aware that critical biography can too easily reduce the writing to 'neurotic distortion', Saunders gives full weight to Ford's conscious 'elaboration and transformation of reality' (I, 9). As he observes, 'Ford's life can only be understood by doing justice to the stories within which he lived and moved' (I, 9). As a result, Ford's writing is placed at the centre of the biography, and Saunders offers a critical engagement with the entire range of Ford's work.

The 're-appraisal' attempted in this collection of essays does not consist of new readings of Ford's most familiar novels. Though these much-discussed works remain points of reference for several contributors, the focus of critical attention has been directed elsewhere. This series of essays aims rather at a critical engagement with some of Ford's neglected works, a demonstration of the variety of his writings, and some consideration of Ford's relationship to his predecessors and contemporaries.

The first four essays consider aspects of Ford's earlier writing, mainly prior to 1914, and the materials and ideas which went into the making of some of his fictions and poems. Tony Davenport explores some of Ford's uses of the stimulus to his imagination provided by Henry James, particularly by James's later stories. Robert Hampson sets some of Ford's fantasy fictions in the context of fictional uses of the supernatural by other late-nineteenth- and early-twentieth-century writers. Pamela Bickley examines the ambiguities of Ford's responses to, and uses of, his pre-Raphaelite ancestry. Paul Skinner reviews Ford's role as poet and considers his poetry in the context of Imagism, Futurism and Vorticism, looking at both his theory and practice as a poet. Appreciation of many of the earlier writings has been distorted by biographical readings of the poems and novels, by insistence on unlocking the *romans à clef* and on identifying poems with their particular occasions. Ford's intellectual processes are more interesting than that, as attempts to unravel the strands of his strategies and registers reveal. To read early Ford alongside Butler, Christina Rossetti, Wells, Chesterton and others is as least as revealing as to convert fiction and poetry back into autobiographical experience.

The last three essays focus on particular works. Vincent Cheng sees *A Call* as a rehearsal for *The Good Soldier* in its treatment of the conflict between public behaviour and private passion and examines Ford's ambivalence about his characters' attitudes. Max Saunders argues for the importance of *The Marsden Case* for an understanding of Ford's development as well as for the interest of its pervasive concern with writing and reading. David Ayers presents a new reading of *The Rash Act* and *Henry for Hugh*, revealing a challenging fusion of naturalism and mythology. Interestingly, as well as expanding our sense of the complexity and depth of Ford's fiction, the essays identify suggestive connections between the different periods and phases of Ford's writing, demonstrating the continuity in Ford's thinking that is in counterpoint with the flexibility of his technical awareness and his experimentation with roles.

NOTES

1. Granville Hicks, 'My Favorite Forgotten Books', *Tomorrow*, 6 (September 1946), 63-4.

2. Walter Allen had written a favourable article on the Tietjens novels earlier that year in the *New Statesman*: Walter Allen, 'Books in General', *New Statesman*, 31 (20 April 1946), 285.

3. *Princeton University Library Chronicle*, 9 (April 1948), 105-65.

4. Robie Macauley, 'The Good Ford', *Kenyon Review*, 11 (Spring 1949), 269-88; reprinted in J. C. Ransome (ed.), *The Kenyon Critics*, 151-69 and as Introduction to *Parade's End*, New York: Alfred A. Knopf, 1950, v-xxii.

5. Kenneth Young, *Ford Madox Ford*, London: Longmans, Green, 1956; George Sampson (ed.), *The Concise Cambridge History of English Literature*, Cambridge: Cambridge University Press, 1961.

6. Robert Green, *Ford Madox Ford: Prose and Politics*, Cambridge: Cambridge University Press, 1981. For a bibliography of critical work on Ford, see David Dow Harvey, *Ford Madox Ford, 1873-1939: A Bibliography of Works and Criticism*, Princeton: Princeton University Press, 1962; rptd. New York: Gordian Press, 1972; Linda Tamkin, 'A Secondary Source Bibliography on Ford Madox Ford, 1962-79' and Rita Malenczyk, 'A Secondary Source Bibliography on Ford Madox Ford, 1979-85' in *Antaeus*, 56 (Spring 1986), 219-30 and 231-44; Michael Longrie, 'A Secondary Source Bibliography on Ford Madox Ford, 1985-1988' in *Contemporary Literature*, 30:2 (Summer 1989), 328-33; and Max Saunders, 'Ford Madox Ford: Further Bibliographies' in *English Literature in Transition, 1880-1920*, 43:2 (2000), 131-205.

7. Ann Barr Snitow, *Ford Madox Ford and the Voice of Uncertainty*, Baton Rouge: University of Louisiana State University Press, 1984, p. 14.

8. R. L. Mégroz, *Joseph Conrad's Mind and Method*, London: Faber & Faber, 1931, p. 167.

9. Jocelyn Baines, *Joseph Conrad: A Critical Biography*, 1960; Harmondsworth: Pelican Books, 1971, pp. 268, 269.

10. Baines, p. 268.

11. Owen Knowles and Gene Moore (eds.), *Oxford Reader's Companion to Conrad*, Oxford: Oxford University Press, 2000, p. 120.

12. Harry T. Moore, *The Life and Works of D. H. Lawrence*, p. 355.

13. Basil Bunting (ed.), *Selected Poems: Ford Madox Ford*, Cambridge, Mass.: Pym-Randall Press, 1971; Max Saunders (ed.), *Ford Madox Ford: Selected Poems*, Manchester: Carcanet Press, 1997.

14. Arthur Mizener, *The Saddest Story: A Biography of Ford Madox Ford*, New York: Harper & Row, 1971; Alan Judd, *Ford Madox Ford*, London: Collins, 1990.

15. Max Saunders, *Ford Madox Ford: A Dual Life*, Volume I, 'The World Before the War'; Volume II, 'The After-War World', Oxford: Oxford University Press, 1996.

FROM *WHAT MAISIE KNEW* TO *THE SIMPLE LIFE LIMITED*: JAMES'S LATE FICTION AND FORD'S SOCIAL COMEDY

Tony Davenport

I

Mr James does not consider that he came into this world to make it any better otherwise than it could be bettered by his observation and the setting down of his observations. He does not, that is to say, expect to improve the world by advocating anything. He merely gives you material. (*Henry James*, 25-6)

Ford's *Henry James* (1914) argues that James was the greatest author of the day, 'valuable to the world' because he was both a mirror of current social life and a perceiver of its invisible tendencies.[1] He goes some way to justifying what may now seem an unusual view of James's late works by reading *The Spoils of Poynton, What Maisie Knew, The Sacred Fount*, and even *The Golden Bowl* as works of social realism. James is the disinterested observer of 'the world we live in', historian of three civilisations, who, unlike writers such as Wells and Chesterton, 'can cast a ray of light into the profound gloom, into the whirl of shadows, of our social agnosticism' (*HJ* 65) without any religious, moral or political axes of his own to grind. Ford recognises that James is selective, and has, like a scientist, become a specialist. Taking over James's own distinction between 'down-town' subjects (the masculine life of the New York business world) and 'up-town' subjects (the mainly feminine life of society, family and home),[2] Ford claims for James the discriminating up-town impressionism which assesses 'all the strivings' without the necessity of close observation of the 'dirty little affairs' of the City which are 'not worth the attention of any intelligent being':

> If Mr James, then, has given us a truthful picture of the leisured life that is founded upon the labours of all this stuff that fills graveyards, then he ... has afforded matter upon which the sociologist ... may build. (*HJ* 61)

The reference to filling graveyards occurs several times in *Henry James* and the idea 'resounds through [Ford's] work with an eerie fascination and abhorrence', as Max Saunders expresses it.[3] One passage it harks back to is the dialogue in *Mr Apollo* where the god exposes the falsity of Parson Todd's self-approving thoughts of how indispensable he has been to the poor by asking him what aspirations all these people have and what becomes of them: '"They – they fill graveyards," he said.'[4] In a similar way Ford sees James exposing the state of society by means of impartial, sardonic observation. He claims that even James's methods, his ambiguities, parentheses, nervous self-corrections and amplifications, are attuned to the society he is registering. As Robert Green puts it, 'Ford associates the perplexities of contemporary life, evanescent and transient, with the very methods James chose to render that world.'[5] The high intelligence of the writing is a contribution to the integrity of the nation's culture and so to the integrity of its business world.

Ford speaks of *The Spoils of Poynton*, *What Maisie Knew* and *The Sacred Fount* as novels primarily about English hypocrisy concerning money and property, adultery and litigation, and his response in his own practice as a novelist to these themes had initially been stronger than to James's intense perceivers, Fleda, Maisie and the narrator of *The Sacred Fount*. But when, significantly close to the time of writing *The Good Soldier*, he came to think about the contribution to *The Spoils of Poynton* of the character of Fleda, he concluded that she serves James's up-town purpose and refines the actions of the other characters: 'a civilising personality introduced into an affair is better than any lawsuit' (*HJ* 36). Ford acquired a greater experience of law-courts than James and was less reluctant to dirty his hands: hence his willingness to go down-town in, for example, *Mr Apollo*, for a court-scene, descriptions of slum-dwellings and the office of the *Daily Outlook*, but it is not always so in Ford's fiction. Family litigation in *The Simple Life Limited* is reported in retrospect, and the city life of the commuting Simple-Lifers is kept off-stage. However, it took longer for Ford to develop the Jamesian perceiver as a focusing device in his observation of social life.

James's registration of shifts of value in the twentieth-century world, of the effects of commercialism, of the decline in delicacy and manners as greater respect is given to money, social display and possession, is even more in evidence in the motifs and situations of his late stories, those printed in the *English Review* and the others collected in *The Finer Grain* (1910).[6] In 'The Jolly Corner' James makes Spencer Brydon meet the other self that he might have become, had he led the down-town life of money and deals. He finds him a horror, 'evil, odious, blatant, vulgar', but the sympathetic woman in the story sees further than that: 'He has been unhappy, he has been ravaged ... he's grim, he's worn – and things have happened to him.'[7] Another up-town view of a down-town New York subject is presented in 'A Round of Visits', where the bitterness of Monteith's discovery that his friend Bloodgood has cheated him drastically changes his sense of life: he feels in charge of 'some horrid alien thing, some violent, scared, unhappy creature whom there was small joy ... in remaining with' (*The Finer Grain*, 140). The black joke of the story (that the only friend who has the time, kindness and intuitive sympathy to listen to his agitation is another twister expecting the police to arrive and using Monteith's betrayed misery to postpone the moment when he must shoot himself) leaves the idea of friendship transformed from loyalty to nervous sympathy in a moment of desperation.

The vulgar freedoms of a society with little respect for social convention are explored in 'Mora Montravers', where James contrasts the suburban respectability of Wimbledon with the suspected loosenesses of Bohemia and the West End. Irony is again the mode: the Traffles' efforts to protect their niece's reputation from her own folly by virtually buying her a husband serve only to convert a rebellious, unmarried Mora Montravers, who may or may not be the artist's mistress, into respectable Mrs Puddick, the artist's wife on the verge of bolting into adultery. In 'The Velvet Glove' James examines the upside-down publishing world of best-sellers and literary lions. His narrator, John Berridge, is a transitory celebrity, author of 'a slightly too fat volume' which has become 'a fifth-act too long play' (*The Finer Grain*, 2); through his uncertain eyes James shows us a handsome young lord and a beautiful princess, figures of Olympian perfection from a Grecian urn, a couple from the world of romance who turn out to be no more than trashy novelist Amy Evans and her insolent upper-class friend trying to get a puff for her latest book.[8] The nearest to a Fordian hero in these stories is the suffering Herbert Dodd, refined, honourable and feeble, in 'The Bench of Desolation', 'alone possessed ... of the secret of sitting still with one's fate' in 'a world of fidgets and starts' (*The Finer Grain*, 257). He is overwhelmed by the aggressive determination of Kate Cookham who screws enough money out of him by threatening a breach of promise action to give herself a life at the expense of his, and then to have the nerve to return to Properley and tell him that it was all for him. James stresses Dodd's abhorrence for the vulgarity of Kate's behaviour:

> There she was, in all the grossness of her native indelicacy, in all her essential excess of will and destitution of scruple. (*The Finer Grain*, 232)

That this masculine model of decency is harried by 'the use on her side of the vulgarest forms known to the law' but eventually protected by an unscrupulous manager of life has many resonances for Ford's own relationships during the Edwardian period, but more significant is Ford's sense of the tale as another instance of James's awareness of 'the world we live in', and of his observation of strong-willed women such as Ida Farange, Kate Cookham and Mrs Gereth, who would lie and cheat for property, and of decent but weak-willed heroes like Owen Gereth, Herbert Dodd and Sir Claude in *What Maisie Knew*.

James saw the point of connection among the five tales he put together to form *The Finer Grain* as 'a central and lively consciousness' involved in 'a tangle of circumstances of which the measure and from which the issue is the vivacity and the active play of the victim's or the victor's sensibility'. It was here that the 'finer grain' was to be seen, in the sensibility of the hero, accessible 'to suspense or curiosity, to mystification or attraction ... to moving experience.' His central figures are all exposed, in different ways, to evidence of the decline of modern manners, instances of vulgarity, treachery, aggression, acquisitiveness, cheap smartness, scorn for convention, but the interest for James is in the moral drama of the activity in 'the sentient, perceptive, reflective part of the protagonist' and in 'the quality of the agitating, the challenging personal *adventure*.'[9] In so far as it is possible to read the stories through Ford's eyes, it would appear that the sensibility of the hero was less immediately interesting to him (at this stage of his development as a novelist, that is) than the novelist's actual observation of social changes and circumstances which provided occasions for adventure. This is particularly clear if one compares James's and Ford's uses of similar social phenomena. So, in 'Crapy Cornelia' James's hero White-Mason is already absorbing evidence on which he will judge the woman he is considering marrying, as he observes her house, with its 'gloss of new money' and its 'general shining immediacy':

> ... the whole place seemed to reflect as never before the lustre of Mrs Worthingham's own polished and prosperous little person – to smile, it struck him, with her smile, to twinkle not only with the gleam of her lovely teeth, but with that of all her rings and brooches and bangles and other gewgaws, to curl and spasmodically cluster as in emulation of her charming complicated yellow tresses, to surround the most animated of pink-and-white, of ruffled and ribboned, of frilled and festooned Dresden china shepherdesses with exactly the right system of rococo curves and convolutions and other flourishes, a perfect bower of painted and gilded and moulded conceits.
> ('Crapy Cornelia', *The Finer Grain*, 192)

White-Mason's preference is for the tone of time, not these bright newnesses, for the gossipy company of the dim, elderly survivor from old New York rather than a restoring marriage to Mrs Worthingham's knowing modernity:

The high pitch of interest, to his taste, was the pitch of history, the pitch of acquired and earned suggestion, the pitch of association, in a word. (*The Finer Grain*, 190)

Ford is interested in the kind of social change that James records, but renders it straight, without the measuring and judging perception of the pained observer, leaving us to judge, for example, Mrs Luscombe's plans for the house, once her mother-in-law is dead:

> What was early Victorian she would sell, replacing it with light, bright, curly objects of furniture after the fashion of what she had been taught to call 'the nouvel art'. From the walls she would have down the heavy, dark sumptuous wall-papers resembling as they did purple and brown damasks and in their place she would paint, distemper, or enamel, in shades of light blue, white or pink. The few Chippendale objects she would retain but she was going to have them varnished, polished and brought up to a pitch of efficient shininess. (*The Simple Life Limited*, 39)[10]

Ford's Jamesian model could as well be the varnishing Brigstocks in *The Spoils of Poynton* but the context of illustrative scenes and encounters and of sketches of ways of life in the case-histories assembled in *The Simple Life Limited* recalls the cumulative effect of the tales in *The Finer Grain*, except that the bright comedy of Ford's 'pitch of efficient shininess' is substituted for the melancholy reflectiveness of James's 'pitch of association'.

To some extent the narrowing sympathies of James in old age could be said to reinforce the fogeyish elements in Ford's outlook.[11] He was obviously in tune with the passages in *The American Scene* where James laments the 'defeat of history' in New York's skyscrapers and elevators and the 'eclipse of manners' in American life, or divines a 'hunger for history' expressed by 'vast, costly empty newness'.[12] But James's stories also encouraged in Ford a riper *comic* awareness of the 'fidgets and starts' of the social and literary world in the late Edwardian and early Georgian period. The familiar scenario of Ford's development as a novelist reduces his early novels to apprentice works[13] which precede *The Good Soldier*, 'the saddest story', into which, for the first time, he put all that he knew about writing. But he did not, in fact, use *all* that he knew. In the period 1900-1914 Ford was also practising a range of comic and satirical techniques, and James was as suggestive a source for these as he was for Dowell and the rest of the quartet of watchers in *The Good Soldier*.

II

James's main target for satire was the vulgarity of the press, featured variously in *The Portrait of a Lady*, *The Reverberator*, *The Bostonians* and so on, but he created a general set-up for comedy and satire elsewhere simply from the antithesis between American and European ways. Ford develops such satirical strategies and stances in most of his early non-historical fiction. In *The Inheritors* he used the dystopia technique of a visitor from another world (another dimension in this case). George Moffat in *The Benefactor* is, like Candide, the central honourable man by whom the folly and greed of others are measured. In *An English Girl* the device is the translation of characters from one environment (England) to another (first shipboard life and then America). In *Mr Apollo* it is the arrival of a supernatural being to inspect life on earth, and in *Ladies Whose Bright Eyes* it is the time-traveller exploring the values of one age in the terms of another. They all look like attempts to put a modern gloss on Jamesian ideas and themes; Ford was looking for angles as well as subjects. None of them is entirely successful, because Ford will try to do too many things at once.

   The Inheritors combines a satirical picture of the contemporary world of literature and journalism with a novel about the hero's fear of loss of control over his life and of political change: there is plenty of material in these themes alone, without the philosophical abstraction generated by the science-fiction situation and the disguised treatment of contemporary political situations in Europe and Africa. In *The Benefactor* a lively observation of the ways of hangers-on and social parasites does not quite slot in to a 'tale of a small circle' about love and renunciation with faint echoes of *Watch and Ward* and *Roderick Hudson*. *An English Girl* is another uncomfortable mixture, this time of James and popular romance fiction: the language of moral analysis and lengthy sentences of qualification are hopelessly at odds with soppy clichés about love and sentiment. Ford's original title, *The Reformers*, his characterisation of the hero as a William Morris Socialist, and the contrast between the vague generosity of this bewildered idealist and the critical precision and assertive achievement of other characters are all connecting points with Ford's own earlier and later novels, as well as with *The American* or *The Bostonians*, but they indicate Ford's failure to decide whether he was writing a parody of James, by reversing James's old European corruptions into new American ones, or a comic exposure of the silliness of social conventions, or a romantic novel about the tensions and oppositions surrounding a love affair. The treatment of Eleanor consequently both undermines and depends on romancer's gush about English womanhood; early on there is some promise that Ford might be going to do for conventional views of pure girlhood what Samuel Butler had done for the sanctities of family life, with some tart observations such as Don's 'If women have ... to lead this splendid, cloistral life, someone's got to provide the investment in Consols to do it on' (*EG* 31). But the Jamesian model Ford is using at this stage in his writing pushes him towards an unsatisfactory renunciation as his ending, and Eleanor ends up no more liberated than Claire de Cintré or Verena Tarrant.

Mr Apollo shows Ford, influenced despite himself by the examples of Wells and Chesterton, beginning to separate out those strands in his own imagination which contribute to the novel of the *Rasselas* type about the 'choice of life' from the moral romance about altruism and the oppressed hero (which will continue to be explored in *A Call*). The portrayal of Alfred and Frances Milne, teachers and thinkers, as displaced members of the former moneyed, powerful classes forced into a debilitating, if useful, life sets up a more persuasive social argument than Ford had managed to articulate in earlier fiction. The

14

meaningfulness of the book as allegory is strongest in the exploration (at the beginning of Part III) of the interweaving in the life of Frances Milne of domestic life, thoughts on education and the composition of poetry: the demonstration of the presence of enlightenment, knowledge and poetry in her life, of Apollo's presence within her, and her recognition of Alfred's need to be comforted and supported, convincingly establish her case to be an 'inheritor', one who carries into a new world the best values of the old. This serious 'condition of life' fable, if Ford had stuck to it, could perhaps accommodate set pieces such as the attack on the press, but the figure of Apollo, who in the strategy of the novel is simply an enabling device, becomes too glamourised, whether one sees him, with Moser, as Ford's picture of himself as 'the Top Toff of all' or, with Max Saunders, as one of Ford's idealisations of Arthur Marwood, while the ending shows a fatal falling for a cheap curtain. [14]

Although Ford went on walking this same tightrope in the satirical novels of the period 1910-14[15] (so much so that Ann Snitow, who gives the best account of Ford as a satirist, can sum up his inconsistencies in the words 'Ford floundered around in a painful spiritual state of unknowing'[16]), he did slowly find a way out of diagrammatic moral satire and allegorical fables towards something closer to a comedy of manners. When he wrote *Henry James*, he was to some extent reviewing his own development as a novelist, his own absorption of James's 'Subjects', 'Temperaments' and 'Methods'.[17] His praise of James's disinterested observation and lack of propagandist intention is an encouragement to the reader to recognise that the element of *roman à clef* in Ford's early fiction gradually became less clear-cut. Greater confidence in writing social comedy and an interesting complexity in fictionalising personal experience both distinguish *The Simple Life Limited*.

III

The Simple Life Limited, published under the pseudonym Daniel Chaucer, has been seen with favour by only a few readers, as in Snitow's description: 'Ford's sunniest and most successful comic novel'.[18] It has, though, almost always been read purely in terms of the personal relationships which Ford was fictionalising. John Batchelor, for instance, judges the novel to be 'an unstructured and angry work' and reads it 'as expressing Ford's *private* feelings about his differences from Conrad'.[19] The portraits of Conrad as Brandetski/Bransdon and of Edward Garnett as Parmont have often been seen as vindictive and the novel's heart. Moser frankly calls it a *roman à clef*, and sees it as Ford's working out the contradictions of his relationships with Conrad and Arthur Marwood.[20] Max Saunders too places it in the context of Ford's private life:

> Out of the estrangement from Marwood, Conrad and Edward Garnett, and also out of his uncertain, aggrieved animosity towards Elsie, came the satirical novels written under the pseudonym of Daniel Chaucer.[21]

However, in analysing the novel later, Saunders takes an appropriately more complex view, recognising that none of the major characters 'represents a single real person'.[22]

Certainly plenty of Ford's own memories are drawn on as raw material. He made use of his reminiscences of the ups and downs in the history of Morris & Co. (recalled in *Ancient Lights*), the various groups of socialists and anarchists in the nineties (recalled in *Return to Yesterday*), and some individuals, such as Prince Kropotkin; added to these is Ford's experience of country life in Romney Marsh, at Limpsfield with the Garnetts, and at the Pent. Country life involved again memories of individuals such as Mrs Pease, the energetic Scottish wife of a Fabian official, in knee-breeches, dragging at the reins of a donkey in a governess-cart containing two little boys, while she commanded Ford to teach Cora Crane to make medieval dresses.[23] By conflating the recent experiences of *English Review* days with the Garnetts' building of 'The Cearne' and the establishment of a community at Limpsfield in the late 1890s,[24] Ford creates a comic milieu which enables him to snipe at pre-Raphaelitism, Socialism, English Fabians and ideas of communal life, English support for Russian political exiles, Conrad's neurotic laziness, the manipulations of literary agents, the unreliability of literary patrons, contemporary novels and plays, and so on. The joke fell rather flat and the disguise of Daniel Chaucer was soon penetrated: 'i.e. Ford Hueffer – a pot boiler and scandalous', scrawled a furious Olive Garnett in her diary a couple of months after publication.[25] Although the allusions to the Conrads and to the Frog's Hole and Limpsfield community are unmistakable, the figures have in fact been variously identified: Gubb as both Ford and the agent J. B. Pinker, Luscombe as Ford and Marwood, and so on.

Though some of the writing is a little careless, *The Simple Life Limited* is, in my view, one of the most entertaining of Ford's pre-1914 books – another being *Ancient Lights*, also published in 1911 and also a partly fictionalised version of his pre-Raphaelite past. Parts of both are very funny, and comedy is, after all, one of Ford's great gifts. The novel is full of detail, expressing a fascination with objects, materials, furniture, clothes, attitudes and physical movements. Ford imagines his characters against a richly pictured background of spaces and colours, textures and decorations. A particularly elaborate instance is the description of Bransdon's loom-room, whose lime-washed, woodsmoke-stained walls are adorned by Rossettian postcard-sized prints produced by Ophelia Bransdon's press:

> They represented mostly outlines of ladies very developed about the hips and obviously with no stays, who leaned their heads back in strained attitudes and saluted doves, the emblems of peace; butterflies, the emblems of the soul; or roses and vines, which are emblems of the beauty and bounteousness of nature. As a rule this figure wore round her head a spiky halo of rays in the midst of which there was generally inscribed the words: 'Sancta Beata Simplicitas!' (*SLL* 52)

It is time the novel was reprinted and made available to readers for whom the Conrad- and Garnett-baiting does not dominate. The relationship between the figures and events of the novel and actual life is, as already suggested, quite complex. If Ford put some part of his conception of himself into the generous, sensible Tory landowner Luscombe, kindly father, considerate husband and son, country gentleman, classicist and sportsman, he can equally be seen in the bewildered, Candide-like figure of Hamnet Gubb, idealist and (as he becomes) small producer. There is something of Ford in the cheerful organiser Everard, and in the wretched Gubb Senior, at least in his role of amanuensis to the great Bransdon. There is a discernible Fordian angle in all parts of the novel, even at the supposed Conradian centre.

The question of the Fordian identity is a familiar and labyrinthine problem. Wells's unkind comment, 'What he is really or if he is really, nobody knows now and he least of all: he has become a great system of assumed personas and dramatized selves', is well illustrated by *The Simple Life Limited*.[26] When he wrote the book he had not yet reached the point of his two later legal changes of name but already the transmutation of Fordie from Ford Hermann Hueffer to Ford H. M. Hueffer and Ford H. Madox Hueffer, plus the German Catholic diversion into Joseph Leopold as part of the Violet Hunt experience, and the publishing disguisings of Fenil Haig, Francis M. Hurd, Ignatz von Aschendrof and now Daniel Chaucer, provide unusually rich evidence of a writer's games with identity, of uncertainty as to who and what he was, what allegiance he should proclaim, what indiscretion he should conceal, and what his name might cost. The collaboration with Conrad, which still leaves the extraordinary literary situation in which two books, *The Inheritors* and *The Nature of a Crime*, which are largely Ford's, are shelved, listed and identified among the works of Conrad, is unique testimony to Ford's willingness to take on the voice of another writer. His subsequent novels provide many less obvious examples of his trying on of stylistic identities, not least in his dashing from one kind of writing to another, but also in his use of pastiche and parody and in his adoption of alternating subservient and satirical stances.

In *The Simple Life Limited* there is a striking major instance of identity shift, as well as several minor ones. The guru Bransdon, spiritual leader of the followers of the Simple Life, is presented first as a grotesque image of the pre-Raphaelite past, with a floating mane of bluish-grey hair, like 'some strange gelatinous creature existing among the weeds and twilight at the bottom of the sea'. One of the best comic scenes (Part II, Chapter III) shows the ethereal artist in his studio, being prepared by his satellite Gubb to be caught unawares by Lady Croydon (a visitor who is inspecting the colony to see if any money can be made out of the idea) in the act of folk-weaving or impromptu dictation of his poetic prose: 'I will hie me to the waste places of the sea...,' he exudes, and 'Mr Bransdon's eyes looked downward so that he had an air of a sort of mystical blindness. "Oh, Ulalune lost!" he chanted, "Girl of the grey eyes and the milk-white feet ..."' Ford has by then filled in some background details of Bransdon's earlier career as ruthless overseer of native railway workers in East Africa, violent and unstable, but this augments the effect of the great man's persona as a careful construct; like Lord Jim, he has made himself an identity and a life, from which the establishment of the Simple Life colony has followed. Ford goes to a lot of trouble to impress on the reader the initial picture of Bransdon, like 'a monstrous idol in the shrine of his loom, framed duskily ... in the rather dim apartment' with 'the appearance of oriental and semi-blind imbecility' and 'eyebrows drooping in similar lines to those of a weeping willow', his large, dim flabbiness set off by the figure of Gubb, 'very pink, bald and shining, holding ready a reporter's notebook and pencil'. The effect combines the studied first impressions of James with the grotesque comedy of the Walrus and the Carpenter, or the rival poets in *Patience*.

Indications of the phoney quality of Bransdon's personality are present throughout. Faced with a genuine rustic (old George grumbling about the water supply and people interfering with what he wants to do with his new bath), Bransdon quickly reverts with Lady Croydon to the language and assumptions of a colonial expatriate. The Countess, who has been nervous about conversing with a great Intellectual, is relieved to discover that he is really 'one of us', which uncomfortably seems to mean a bullying fascist with a history of brutality to the labouring 'natives'. He is soon ordering silk shirts and new suits and changing his appearance into a new macho style of shorn locks and manly fisticuffs,

19

and planning with theatrical manager Everard to write up his African experiences for the commercial theatre. Even so and even after his rejection of 'this Simple Life yap' (*SLL* 251) and a reversion to 'his old vocabulary which was half that of the mercantile quarterdeck and half that of American bar-loafers' (*SLL* 254), we are still unprepared for Bransdon's sudden switch to man of action in Part IV, Chapter IX, where he behaves as a practical, vigorous leader of men, rescuing clothes, manuscripts, people from fire, directing others with clear authority and giving the impression of casting off a disguise and exposing the weakness of Gubb, who earlier had seemed the stronger character. The final view of him brings back his self-importance and his phoniness. Transformed again into a successful playwright, author of the long-running *The White Man's Burden* and now writing a play about the Stock Exchange, he appears in top hat and Spanish cloak with eye-glass as man-about-town and potential husband to the Dowager Countess Croydon. 'Look here,' he protests at the end of the book to Hamnet Gubb, whose explanation of his own views on life threatens to draw too much of the limelight, 'I'm not taking half the share in this conversation that is due to my dignity and years'. Hamnet characterises him as 'you unscrupulous old artist', likely to shift and change from one phase to another, and likely to exploit Hamnet's version of the Simple Life and romanticise it:

> 'When you've got into another romantic phase you'll write about me as a young faun, as something that has ... identified itself with Nature ... the heartbeat of Nature. That's the sort of thing, isn't it, old boy?... only you'd turn me into a nigger in primordial South Africa.' (*SLL* 388)

Whatever digs at Conrad or W. H. Hudson may be identified in this, the overall quality of the picture of Bransdon goes beyond caricature of an individual. Ford has created a comic Protean artist, and within the wavering outline of this lazy/active, bearded/clipped, ugly/handsome, shabby/flamboyant balloon may be discerned both Ford's sense of himself as a writer capable of changing from poet to historian, romancer to critic, and aspects that he saw in others, including James.[27]

Both 'The Velvet Glove' and *The Simple Life Limited* are written in the spirit of 'Where are the eagles and the trumpets?' If James's over-lionised hero 'poor Berridge' is a Prufrock in the making, Ford creates in Bransdon and Gubb a pair of outpourer and catcher who turn literature into a commercialised parody of past ideas of creative art. James's highlighting of the bathos of the modern literary world is through the language of epic and allusions to Greek myth and echoes of Keats; Ford's is by means of ironic allusions to *Hamlet*. Ford's Ophelia is no ethereal heroine declining into madness, but a sturdy, noisy, protesting girl who strains Mrs Luscombe's Parisian lace to bursting and whose singing ambitions tend towards appearing in a West End musical rather than a pathetic death scene. Little Hamnet Gubb, the solitary contemplative, who spends much of the novel away at the equivalent of Wittenberg, also returns from his studies to find a former love changed, the father-figure gone and the money-changers in the temple:

'This is what I find! I went away to study the world. I found it commercially horrible, distasteful. I returned to this place thinking to find a green coolness and pure minds. I find the world has crept in here, too. Everything is greed! Everything is jealousy! Everything is self-conscious! Everything is a weariness!' (*SLL* 316)

Just in case we have not registered the comparison, Everard, who finds Hamnet sitting on a milestone, remarks 'you only want a skull and you'd do for Hamlet' (*SLL* 317). Hamnet's disgust with the world is more akin, though, to that of another contemplator of skulls, Scythrop Glowry in *Nightmare Abbey*, rather than a tragic struggle to preserve honour and integrity. He is a post-Romantic limited survivor who is allowed the last word in the novel and who answers at least some of its (and Hamlet's) questions:

'The only rule of the Simple Life is not to have any rules at all. You just live and see where you come out ... If you think about Life it isn't Life. If you

21

think about the sort of man to model yourself on, you aren't a man. You're a trained rat.' (*SLL* 384)

Everard combines the roles of Player-King and Fortinbras. His theatrical repertoire shows tragical-comical-historical-pastoral turned into:

> ... terrific conflagrations in strictly fireproof watermills, with a backcloth representing a snowy landscape, and the villain's deserted wife and three deserted children crying vainly for help from the roof as it fell in; honest declarations of manly faith and virtues uttered by heroes with strong North-country accents; ladies with very huge feathered hats ... whose feet, though their hearts were extravagantly in the right place, had a tendency to take the wrong turnings ... (*SLL* 158)

His getting on with things and bringing order out of chaos earns Hamnet's recognition in him of the fulfilment of an ideal of life: 'to know the life you like and to have the courage to lead it ... He's not self-conscious' (*SLL* 384). The irony of this simple fulfilment's being found in a stage-manager of pretences and shows is explicitly directed at the supposed leaders, Bransdon and his Horatio (Gubb), who without specific correspondence have some characteristics of Claudius and Polonius. The parallels are not forced and other strands of plot and satire form cross-currents with these glances back to Shakespeare, but such moments as Hamnet's and young Brandetski's quarrel over Ophelia in a deserted gravel-pit in the moonlight (Part IV, Chapter VI) invite recognition of a Laertes-like aspect in Brandetski, the wild revolutionary, and the scene carries echoes of the gravediggers, too:

> 'Yet, what are all my needs in life? Six feet of the clay soil of the cottage that I lie upon ... One six foot is as good to me as another.' (*SLL* 328)

Thus Hamnet, while Brandetski is given some language reminiscent of Hamlet's own:

'... that I may not strangle you I will move myself to a distance. I will go and drink water at the spring and pray for the consummation of what I desire. All these days I am fevered, I am torn with agony ...' (*SLL* 328-9)

These allusions are constantly placed in a comic context by the farcical elements in the plot; the quarrel of the two young men is nothing to the self-important Ophelia who is to marry the honest vulgarian Everard.

The comic technique in the novel varies. The book begins with a confrontation, and a number of other such scenes are scattered throughout. The striking opening with Luscombe and his young son within and the bedraggled Hamnet and Ophelia outside getting soaked through their awful homespun grey suits sets a tone of crisp downrightness once the dialogue starts.

> 'We ought,' [Hamnet] said, 'to inform you that we object to the abominable institution of marriage. We were married yesterday morning, but we desire to enter the strongest possible protest.'
>
> Mr Luscombe raised his eyebrows, whistled between his teeth, and smiled in a slightly puzzled manner.
>
> 'Well, well,' he said, 'I've heard of repenting at leisure, but I never heard of a couple who found out their mistake so soon.' (*SLL* 6)

The basic terms of debate or antithesis, between pretentious opinions on one side and common-sense practicality on the other, are declared. But from the antithesis complications are interestingly developed. The first impression of Bohemian youth challenging a country-house-owning Establishment begins to acquire depth when that Establishment itself proves to be an example of society in flux: the family history of the Luscombes suggests the aftermath of some Hardyesque fiction, such as *The Return of the Native*, a tale of adultery, litigation, country hostility. The absurdities of the 'Simple Life' are set against the cross-currents of class rivalry, money-grubbing and malice which we have to accept as the 'real' condition of English social life. The scenes of confrontation are woven together with sketches of careers and backgrounds and descriptions of places and rooms by which ways of life are represented.

23

Luscombe, Mrs Luscombe, Parmont, Bransdon, Gubb and later the Earl and Countess of Croydon, the Lee family, Mr Major the architect, Everard and the revolutionary Brandetski, together with other brief identifications, are all presented as case histories which illustrate shifts in contemporary British and European social standards, politics and attitudes; the comic light in which they are displayed offers them as instances of confusions, opportunities and quirks, disguises and hypocrisies, exploitations by others and flauntings of self. The cumulative impression is eventually more striking than the satirical effect of individual portraits.

Ford is multifarious and wide-ranging in all his satirical novels, and he never in these books suggests anything like James's concentration and narrow focus. Nevertheless one recognises structural features which Ford learned from James: the linked chains of action and character from *What Maisie Knew*, the succession of focal scenes from *The Spoils of Poynton* or *The Awkward Age*, the conveying of character through surroundings and possessions. So, for example, Part I, Chapter V uses the characteristic late Jamesian technique of starting with a piece of direct speech (Parmont asking Bransdon about his sale of Frog's Cottages), which is then 'gone behind' in an explanation of place, characters, situation, before a return ten pages later to the question with which the chapter began. Again Part III consists of only three chapters, each a set-piece complete in itself in which are visible resemblances to both James and Shaw. In the first of these Ford makes a shift to the grand house of the Earl of Croydon (ironically built to the same Gilbert Scott design as the local workhouse) and dramatises the visit of Mrs Lee and her ghastly children through the eyes of the servants; the contemptuous view of the Simple Life from the Earl's Marxist footman is that 'it's another of those bourgeois manifestations of Tolstoyism' (*SLL* 189). The Shavian gimmick bears fruit, as the chapter ends with the folly of the aristocratic view which thinks the Lee children's behaviour is sensibly based on educational principle and sees even the conduct of the perverse donkey as evidence that 'These people are so very practical' (*SLL* 196). The second chapter is less broadly comic, a dialogue for four in Germany, in which the degree of social rebellion manifested by the mainly bourgeois Simple Lifers is further diminished by comparison with political revolt and theoretical issues. Ford hits off one attitude against another, giving to Parmont a definition of idealism: 'to hate conventions and love beauty; to hate commercialism and live a frugal life; to be sceptical of all pretensions and to seek to harm nobody' (*SLL* 212-13). To Hamnet is given expression of a non-political quietism while Miss Stobhall voices the sturdy Fabian arguments for corporate life, which is the main object of the novel's criticism, as Ford's comic quips indicate. Miss Stobhall's 'idea of enjoyment in life was to get a quiet evening to herself to read Fabian tract No.32 by Mr Sidney Webb on "The Breakdown of Individualism"' (*SLL* 213). The third chapter focuses on the increasing commercialism and worldliness of the community, with the fight with the local inhabitants which leads to Bransdon's change of appearance and attitude. This third section of the novel is a carefully constructed Fordian version of James's 'scenario' method.

The fourth and last part of the book is, as elsewhere in Ford's fiction, the least effective. The force of the comedy is dissipated in a frantic build-up of incident to the tragi-farcical climax of Brandetski's arson and suicide – *progression d'effet* run riot. But there is a good scene between Gubb and Luscombe (Part IV, Chapter II), in which Gubb over-reaches himself with his plans for a bigger and better colony. Ford has some fun here imagining Gubb's idea of a wholesome library:

'Our library ... will contain only such serious books as will lead to improve the tone of the mind of the readers ... Fiction we shall entirely banish except perhaps for the works of Richardson and for one or two Utopian novelists such as Mr Wells, Mr Galsworthy and Mr Upton Sinclair. We desire, above all things, to communicate to our fellow workers a tone of earnestness and of serious attention to the problems of life.' (*SLL* 264)

The ethos of a Simple Life community (and presumably of the Garden City, which, through the Croydons' desire to cash in on the movement, he gets the chance to control) is expressed as:

> ... sane healthy pleasures, cultivating alike the Arts and the face of the earth, not only making a little oasis of perfect beauty in the midst of the grim sordidness of modern life, but beautiful in itself and in all its members, pointing out ... the only thinkable road towards social regeneration. (*SLL* 267)

However, the altruist is not, as George Moffat in *The Benefactor* was, endlessly capable of sacrifice; the terms in which Luscombe expresses his rejection of Gubb are indicative of Ford's less extreme, more plausible terms of thought:

> 'I am not a lunatic. I am not even a philanthropist ... I am just a country landowner anxious to do my duty unobtrusively.' (*SLL* 271)

Gubb inevitably has an answer:

> 'I took you for a straightforward and noble man. I find you just as spotted with the commercial greed of the age as all your fellows.' (*SLL* 276)

The deflation of Gubb's bubble of pretence is really the end of the Simple Life as a commercial limited company, and Ford could have wound up his novel with the sort of antithesis between pretension and common-sense which has been the basis of the comedy from the start:

> 'I have eaten husks and crusts like the prodigal son.'
> 'Oh come,' said Gerald, 'you're a vegetarian anyhow.' (*SLL* 277)

Although the stories of the two novels are very different, in terms of overall effect, there is a similarity between *The Simple Life Limited* and *What Maisie Knew*.[28] James conveyed a general sense of society as a precarious game, in which raffish, hard-up adventurers skate dashingly between the decaying decencies of life lived within one's means and the confines of old respectabilities, and the indulgences and profits of catching hold of the coat-tails of the *nouveaux riches*. Ford similarly compiles a composite picture of society, somewhat in the style of his grandfather's famous painting *Work*.[29] The landowning Tory Luscombes, decent enough but tarnished by scandal, extravagance and class-consciousness; the late Victorian, Gothicized aristocrats, the Croydons, hanging on to their possessions by chasing chances of success and financial gain; the bourgeois commuters pretending to be simple craftspeople and noble savages; Bransdon and Gubb exploiting credulity in quest of reputation and money – these, together with the minor characters, the contrast of the actual country people, grumbling and resentful, and of political revolutionaries, suspicious and dangerous, amount to a more important aspect of the novel than the personal jibes. The idea of the Simple Life provides a good central joke and holds the novel together far more surely than the weak stories of *Mr Apollo*, *The New Humpty-Dumpty* or *Mr Fleight*, though they too are designed as pictures of 'the world we live in'. At the end of the tale Hamnet has, like Maisie, learned enough to reject the values of the older generation, simple or otherwise, and to create wonder at what he knows. Ford too impresses by what he knows, both in the precision of his depictions and in the variety and invention of his comic situations. Before sadness and bewilderment took over to stamp the Fordian hero and Ford's literary persona, *The Simple Life Limited* expresses just as characteristic an exuberant independence, and, through the mouth of Hamnet Gubb, a typical Fordian view of the best way to exist: 'to know the life you like and to have the courage to lead it' (*SLL* 384). When he came to write *Parade's End*, among the qualities which he could draw from his mental store-cupboard was a practised gift for comedy and the resilience that goes with it.

NOTES

1. Ford Madox Hueffer, *Henry James*, London: Martin Secker, dated 1913, but not published until early 1914, hereafter referred to in citations as *HJ*.

2. Preface to Volume XVIII of the New York Edition, containing *Daisy Miller*, etc. New York: Scribner, 1909.

3. *HJ* 11 and 140; Max Saunders, *Ford Madox Ford: A Dual Life*, Oxford: Oxford University Press, 1996, Volume I, p. 66.

4. *Mr Apollo*, Part I, Chapter IV. This, in turn, repeats an earlier appearance of the idea and phrase in *SL*, p. 142, as Robert Hampson points out to me; see also *The Inheritors* Ch.18. Later the idea becomes part of Valentine's memory of Tietjens: 'she had, indeed, once heard Tietjens say that humanity was made up of exact and constructive intellects on the one hand and on the other of stuff to fill graveyards' (*SDN* Pt.2, IV).

5. Robert Green, *Ford Madox Ford: Prose and Politics*, Cambridge: Cambridge University Press, 1981, p. 72.

6. Henry James, *The Finer Grain*, London: Methuen & Co.Ltd., 1910, contained 'The Velvet Glove', 'Mora Montravers', 'A Round of Visits', 'Crapy Cornelia' and 'The Bench of Desolation'. In the *English Review* Ford published 'The Jolly Corner (1st issue, Dec.1908), 'The Velvet Glove' (Mar.1909), 'Mora Montravers' (Aug./Sept.1909) and 'A Round of Visits' (Apr./May 1910).

7. 'The Jolly Corner', first published in book form in Volume XVII of the New York Edition, *The Altar of the Dead*, New York: Scribner, 1909, pp. 433-85: quotations from p. 477 and p. 485.

8. The story, referred to by James during composition as 'The Top of the Tree', was obliquely (and later disguisedly) related to Edith Wharton's *The Fruit of the Tree* (1907). See Philip Horne (ed.), *Henry James: A Life in Letters*, London: Allen Lane, The Penguin Press, 1999, pp. 469-71.

9. The quotations are from James's description written for the publisher, printed in Leon Edel and L. H. Powers (eds), *The Complete Notebooks of Henry James*, New York and London: Oxford University Press, 1987, p. 577.

10. *The Simple Life Limited*, London: John Lane, 1910, by 'Daniel Chaucer', hereafter referred to in citations as *SLL*. It was actually published in early 1911.

11. As seen, for example, in the political and social commentaries published in the *English Review* under the heading 'The Month', to which Ford contributed more than anyone else. Some of the essays by friends and associates ring a similar chime: e.g. R. B. Cunninghame Graham on 'Aspects of the Social Question', *English Review* 1 (Dec. 1908) comparing contemporary society to the late Roman Empire when 'everything was breaking down, and though intelligent people saw that this was the case, no one could propose a remedy.' See Ralph Herman Ruedy, *Ford Madox Ford and the English Review*, Duke Univ. Ph.D. (Xerox University Microfilms, Ann Arbor, Michigan, 1976), Chapter 4.

12. Henry James, *The American Scene*, London: Chapman and Hall Ltd., 1907, pp. 113, 129, 183. Ford was reading it in September 1907 (Saunders, Vol. I, p. 230).

13. Ford can surely not, without some sense of irony, have quoted (*HJ* 106-7) James's account in *French Poets and Novelists* (1884) of Balzac's early writings, to the effect that before he was thirty Balzac 'had published, under a variety of pseudonyms, some twenty long novels, veritable Grub Street productions, written in sordid Paris attics, in poverty, in perfect obscurity. No writer ever served a more severe apprenticeship to his art, or lingered more hopelessly at the ladder base of fame.'

14. Thomas C. Moser, *The Life in the Fiction of Ford Madox Ford* Princeton, NJ: Princeton University Press, 1980, p. 74; Saunders, Vol. I, p. 209.

15. That is *The Simple Life Limited* (1910/11); *The New Humpty-Dumpty* (1912); *Mr Fleight* (1913).

16. Ann Barr Snitow, *Ford Madox Ford and the Voice of Uncertainty*, Baton Rouge & London: Louisiana State University Press, 1984, p. 139.

17. These are the titles Ford gave to the chapters of *HJ*.

18. Snitow, p. 144.

19. John Batchelor, *The Edwardian Novelists*, London: Duckworth, 1982, p. 115.

20. Moser, p. 91.

21. *The New Humpty-Dumpty* was also published as by 'Daniel Chaucer'; Saunders Vol. I, pp. 274-5.

22. Saunders, Vol. I, p. 322.

23. *RY* in *Memories and Impressions*, edited by M. Killigrew, (Bodley Head Ford, Vol.

V), London, etc., 1971, pp. 196-7. [Published in USA as *Your Mirror to My Times: The Selected Autobiographies and Impressions of Ford Madox Ford*]

24. See the account in G. Jefferson, *Edward Garnett*, London: Jonathan Cape, 1982, Chapters 2 and 3.

25. Moser, pp. 91-8.

26. H. G. Wells, *Experiment in Autobiography*, first published 1934, reissued London, Faber and Faber, 1984, Vol. II, p. 617.

27. Another aspect of Bransdon is the idea of his gradual emergence from the role of spiritual leader of the Simple Life movement as a recovery from a nervous breakdown, triggered by a blow on the head (*SLL* 245 ff.). Ford was completing the book early in 1910, a period of marital turmoil, including his short spell in prison: Snitow and Saunders both see a therapeutic element of distancing in the novel (see Saunders, Vol. I, pp. 321-3). Ironically at this same time (January 1910 onwards) Henry James was suffering a major breakdown in health.

28. The grip of this novel of James on Ford's imagination is most famously indicated by his account of how he started to write *Parade's End*: 'Nothing was further from my thoughts than writing about the late war. But ... for several days more I lost myself in working out an imaginary war-novel on the lines of *What Maisie Knew*.' (*IWN* 162 [New York: Ecco Press, 1984]). See also Mizener's note on the echoing of *What Maisie Knew* in *The Good Soldier* (Arthur Mizener, *The Saddest Story: A Biography of Ford Madox Ford*, Cleveland: World Publishing, 1971; London: Bodley Head, 1972, p. 603, n.47). Among other persistent echoes of James the influence of 'The Jolly Corner' is visible as late as 1928 when Ford wrote *When the Wicked Man*.

29. Ford Madox Brown's *Work* places navvies at the centre of his picture, but surrounds them with a range of figures, representing aspects of the middle and upper classes; the painting is in the Manchester City Art Gallery.

TRAVELLERS, DREAMERS AND VISITORS:
FORD AND FANTASY

Robert Hampson

I

In his seminal work, *The Fantastic*, Tzvetan Todorov suggested two characteristics of the genre: 'First, the text must oblige the reader ... to hesitate between a natural and supernatural explanation of the events described. Second, this hesitation may also be experienced by a character'.[1] *Ladies Whose Bright Eyes*, one of Ford's most finished and economic fictions, deftly fulfils both these requirements.[2] Its central character, an engineer turned publisher, William Sorrell, finds himself, after a railway accident, apparently back in fourteenth-century England. To begin with, he assumes his experience is a dream:

> 'When I wake up,' he said to himself, 'I wonder if I shall remember all this. It's the flying dream, of course ...' (*LWBE* 45)[3]

But the time-jump and the shift in focalisation between the railway accident at the end of Chapter 2 and the introduction of Lady Blanche and her fourteenth-century world at the start of Chapter 3 – with the consequently delayed re-introduction of Sorrell – gives this medieval world an existence independent of him, that prevents the reader from readily acquiescing in his confident interpretation.[4] The text simultaneously activates a 'natural' reading (in terms of dream-experience) and a 'supernatural' reading (in terms of time-travelling). Other elements in these opening chapters have accordingly an ambivalent status: Sorrell's 'knack of picking up languages' (*LWBE* 16) and his skill in horse-riding can be read as either the contents of his consciousness that shape and direct his 'dream' or as proleptic explanations of his adaptation to the alien world to which he has been 'supernaturally' transported. Sorrell's thoughts about his chance of a knighthood and about 'what a bully time' he might have, if he 'could be thrown right back into the Middle Ages', can similarly be read as either the stimulus for, or ironically proleptic of, the experiences that follow. On the other hand, Mrs Egerton's story of the Tamworth-Egerton crucifix 'carried to Tamworth by a converted Greek slave ... dressed only in a linen shift' (*LWBE* 24), who proved to have 'gifts of prophecy', predicting 'steam-engines and people being able to speak to each other a hundred miles apart and their flying in the air like birds' (*LWBE* 25), introduces a genuine enigma. Sorrell's first appearance in the fourteenth-century landscape 'trotting along the path in a white shift' (*LWBE* 37), 'uttering the words "Egerton" and "Tamworth"' (*LWBE* 45) and carrying the Tamworth-Egerton crucifix, offers a solution to this problem of prophecy but only by introducing a second supernatural explanation: the fantasy of an escape from the linear ordering of time.[5]

Sorrell acts like one of H. G. Wells's scientific protagonists who finds himself in an alien environment. Like the Time Traveller or Prendick in *The Island of Dr Moreau* or Cavor in *The First Men in the Moon*, he generates various hypotheses about the nature of the new world in which he finds himself. After he is compelled to conclude that this 'isn't a dream' (*LWBE* 48), Sorrell decides that he 'must have escaped from a lunatic asylum' (*LWBE* 49) into a remote area of Salisbury Plain. His attempt to read subsequent events as an uncommonly scrupulous re-enactment of 'the legend of the Greek slave' (*LWBE* 71) produces the delightful comedy of his anachronistic responses: his desire to 'borrow a pair of trousers ... and get up to London by the first train' (*LWBE* 53); his urge to 'write to the papers' about the display of corpses on gibbets (*LWBE* 53). As in *The Fifth Queen*, Ford exploits the gap between reader comprehension and character comprehension, but here for purely comic effect. However, once Sorrell concludes that he is 'not only in the middle of Salisbury Plain' but also 'in the middle of the Middle Ages' (*LWBE* 97), he and the narrative settle into the feuds and politics of fourteenth-century England, until, in Parts IV and V, both hesitate between vividly-apprehended passages of natural description after the manner of W. H. Hudson, which assert the reality of the fourteenth-century world:

> The owl, turning at the bottom of the field, floated slowly back, ghostlike amidst the mists along the dark shadows of the woodside, searching for such small mice and frogs as the evening called to their avocations in the grasses. (*LWBE* 251-2)

and, on the other hand, increasingly powerful intimations of another reality:

> Lying upon his back and looking into the darkness, Mr Sorrell was aware of sounds and glimpses of sights. It was as if very dimly he saw about him the shadows of white walls. A drilling sound went on. Above him the shapes of white-dressed women, as indistinct as, in the twilight, are the shadows of poplars, seemed to advance and to recede, now from this side, now from that. (*LWBE* 259)

This leads Sorrell to consider the possibility that 'the ages superimposed themselves the one over the other' (*LWBE* 302). Sorrell's experience recalls Henry Adams's account of the Marches as an area where 'time-sequences became interchangeable':

> As one lay on the slope of the Edge, looking sleepily through the summer haze towards Shrewsbury or Cader Idris or Caer Caradoc or Uriconium, nothing suggested sequence. The Roman road was twin to the railroad ... The shepherds of Caractacus or Offa, or the monks of Buildwas, had they approached where he lay in the grass, would have taken him only for another and tamer variety of Welsh thief. They would have seen little to surprise them in the modern landscape unless it were the steam of a distant railway ...[6]

In opposition to this, however, the end of the novel asserts linear temporality, foregrounded through a concern with Lee-Egerton ancestors and descendants. But with Charles Lee-Egerton as the end of the line, the implications are clearly of degeneration rather than progress:

33

> He was tall, slight, fair – very much like what Sir William himself must have looked like at that age ... But with a weak chin and no air of purpose ... (*LWBE* 341)

This accords with Ford's view of London's 'leisure class' as expressed in *The Soul of London*: 'their ancestors, their family, their *gens*, have worked too much for them: they are left without the need to labour' (*SL* 118-9). And without labour, as Wells had suggested through the Eloi in *The Time Machine*, 'our minds decay, our bodies atrophy, it is all over with us in this world' (*SL* 118). The opposition between these two views of time remains unresolved.[7]

In writing *Ladies Whose Bright Eyes*, Ford was unavoidably conscious of the nostalgia for the medieval of the Pre-Raphaelites.[8] In *Ancient Lights* he had noted:

> Between them, Madox Brown and Rossetti invented a queer and quaint sort of medievalism that was realistic always as long as it could be picturesque. Morris, Swinburne, and Burne-Jones however invented the gorgeous glamour of medievalism. (*AL* 133)

By contrast, his account of medieval noble life emphasises not only the dirt and cold ('The flagstones were disgustingly dirty, and there must be a tremendous draught from all the unglazed windows', *LWBE* 90) but also the smells – whether from decomposing corpses hanging from gibbets (*LWBE* 48) or from 'the slaughter of beasts and of cookery' (*LWBE* 92). Similarly, while Sorrell expects life in the Middle Ages to be 'a simple affair' (*LWBE* 77), what he in fact encounters is a complex political struggle between church and nobles (and within both church and nobility) and, everywhere, a concern with legal argument and legal niceties. In the 1911 version, when Sorrell regains consciousness in the twentieth century, his disgust with the modern world (epitomised by his knighthood for publishing encyclopaedias rather than for chivalric feats of arms) prompts his plan 'to buy the village of Winterburne St. Martin' and 'restore the old farmhouse until it resembled the little castle it had once been' so that he and Dionissia can resume their life there that had ended so abruptly in the fourteenth century. In the 1935 text, this final section is completely re-written: the farmhouse is to be demolished to make way for an air-station, and Sir William and Dionissia prepare to leave for the USSR, where people are 'beginning a new civilisation and certainly with a brilliant faith' (*LWBE* 350). Instead of a purely-personal 'adventure' in a rural retreat, Sorrell's re-education ends in commitment to the cause of 'civilisation' and the future.[9]

Ford acknowledged that *Ladies Whose Bright Eyes* was suggested by Twain's *A Connecticut Yankee at King Arthur's Court*. Twain's frame-tale introduces the idea that Ford's narrative also turns upon: not 'transmigration of souls' but 'transposition of epochs – and bodies'.[10] The 'curious stranger' whom Twain meets in Warwick Castle had, like Sorrell, received a bang on the head, and, as a result, had apparently travelled into the past. Like Sorrell, he at first tries to interpret his new experiences in terms of the circus, the asylum and dreaming. There, however, the similarities end. Hank Morgan has quite different qualifications from Sorrell:

> My father was a blacksmith, my uncle was a horse doctor, and I was both, along at first. Then I went over to the great arms factory and learned my real trade ... learned to make everything – guns, revolvers, cannon, boilers, engines, all sorts of labor-saving machinery. Why, I could make anything a body wanted ... and if there wasn't any quick new-fangled way to make a thing, I could invent one ... (*CY* 36)

Morgan asserts the civilisation of the nineteenth century (specifically, the magic of industrial technology) against the civilisation of the earlier period, and he affirms 'the American way' (republicanism, democracy, 'enterprise') against European monarchy, feudalism and superstition. For most of the narrative, he sees himself as 'a giant among pigmies, a man among children' (*CY* 60) or as an American settler among 'white Indians' (*CY* 53). This colonialist attitude towards the past is also implicit in his first piece of magic: the trick based on prior knowledge of an eclipse that Captain Good exploits so effectively to impress the Kukuanas in *King Solomon's Mines*.[11] Having gained a position of authority and influence, Morgan then quietly works to subvert the host culture: he surveys and maps the kingdom; he mints a new coinage ('nickels, dimes, quarters, and half-dollars', *CY* 131); he develops a communications network of telegraph, telephone and railway; he develops various industries as 'the iron and steel missionaries of my future civilisation' (*CY* 101); he establishes a 'military academy' to create a cadre of technocrats loyal to himself; and, above all, he develops more and more sophisticated weaponry. Before very long, knight errants have become travelling salesmen, and the Round Table has been transformed into a 'stock-board' with Lancelot as a 'bearish' president. Like *Nostromo*, though perhaps less consciously, Twain's novel contains a detailed picture of imperialism and its mode of operation.[12]

Twain's initial impulse was a burlesque of Malory's *Morte d'Arthur*, but the burlesque of chivalric romance developed into a polemic against feudal laws and institutions.[13] In particular, the narrative worked to expose both the absurdity of 'royalty' and the way that the existence of a 'royal family' underwrites a system of privilege and structured inequality. This, in turn, produced a division in Morgan's character and function: he is both a crude American businessman, treated with some degree of irony, a forerunner of Sinclair Lewis's Babbitt, and also the humanitarian emancipator of the oppressed English.[14] Quite apart from the hostility to Catholicism (which Dan Beard's illustrations emphasised), Ford would no doubt have been struck by the novel's apparent celebration of American business values and (inescapably after 1914) by the novel's alignment of those values with weaponry and war.[15] Morgan's education was an initiation into the military-industrial complex, and the novel's climax brings a modern Armageddon to sixth-century chivalry in a landscape that anticipates Passchendaele and the Somme:

> The thirteen gatlings began to vomit death into the fated ten thousand. They halted, they stood their ground a moment against that withering deluge of

fire, then they broke, faced about and swept toward the ditch like chaff before a gale. A full fourth part of their force never reached the top of the lofty embankment ... (*CY* 404)

As early as *When Blood Is Their Argument* (1915), Ford had articulated his opposition to 'materialism, militarism' (*WBTA* xi); in *Between St. Dennis and St. George* (1915), he contrasts the materialism and militarism of Prussia to the 'civilisation of altruism and chivalry' (*BSDSG* 222) of Provence; and in *Provence* (1935), he works out his vision of the 'earthly Paradise' (*Provence* 19) in opposition to 'Industrialism, the Commercial Spirit and Puritanism' (*Provence* 84). In *Great Trade Route* (1937), Ford developed further his advocacy of the 'civilisation of the Mediterranean' against 'the murder and rapine of us conquering Nordics' (*GTR* 23). Ford's travels in North America, which form the basis of this book, lead to a critical engagement with 'the American Technocrat' and an apprehension of genocidal tendencies in North American culture. Given the revised ending of *Ladies Whose Bright Eyes*, it is interesting to note Ford's citing of Lenin on the small producer (*GTR* 79) and his contemplation of the Soviet model: 'if the Russian Soviet really puts its trust in hammers and sickles I would willingly say that I was for the USSR' (*GTR* 224). Ford, however, fears that the USSR, like America, really puts its trust in the Machine, and, in the end, his nostalgia for pre-capitalist modes of production and exchange leads to his sympathy for 'the quasi-feudal system of the great plantations' of the South and a Poundian celebration of Jefferson. The 'wiping out' of 'the gentle, beautiful and highly-cultured feudal civilisation of the Troubadours by the North French' (*GTR* 322) becomes a subject-rhyme for the destruction of 'the civilisation of Virginia' in the Civil War (*GTR* 323). 'Applied science' means for Ford the manufacture of armaments (*Provence* 307), and, in contrast to Twain, 'chivalry' encodes for him a concern for human life as opposed to the destruction of civilian populations through 'total war'.

II

For Todorov the literature of the fantastic was 'the uneasy conscience of the positivist nineteenth century'.[16] Certainly, as Stephen Prickett has shown, the fantastic constituted an important strand in nineteenth-century literature, arising from the popularity of the Gothic, an interest in folk and fairy tales, a renewed feeling for the numinous and/or an opposition to prevailing social values and conditions.[17] This can be traced from Coleridge's 'The Rime of the Ancient Mariner' through the use of 'other worlds' (in Victorian fantasies as diverse as Kingsley's *The Water Babies*, Lewis Carroll's *Alice* books, and George MacDonald's *Lilith: a romance*) to the turn-of-the-century romances of the future.[18] In his 1906 Preface to the second edition of *A Crystal Age*, Hudson observes that romances of the future 'are born of a very common feeling – a sense of dissatisfaction with the existing order of things, combined with a vague faith in or hope of a better one to come'.[19] The hero of *A Crystal Age*, like Morgan and Sorrell, receives a knock on the head which renders him unconscious for hundreds of years (with only a little damage to his tweed suit). The world he awakes to is a pre-urban, pre-industrial 'simple life', created by the survivors of some unspecified scientifically-produced disaster. They live in self-supporting vegetarian communes – based, as Ruth Tomalin notes, 'on the beehive, headed by a single fertile couple' – and in Edenic relations with birds and animals.[20] The narrative makes much of Smith's disorientation in this new world, and the reader at first hesitates between reading it as past or future, but such hesitations are subordinated to Hudson's realization of this society. Similarly, while there is implicit criticism of science and of inherited wealth, the emphasis falls rather on the celebration of the natural world and artistic activity. Both costumes and art-work seem Pre-Raphaelite in inspiration ('with loosened dark golden-red hair and amber-coloured garments fluttering in the wind, stood a graceful female figure'; *The Crystal Age* 45), but it is Hudson the naturalist who produces the detailed and epiphanic visions of nature.

As David Miller suggests, the Crystal Age concern with transcendence (as represented by their art), their harmony with nature and their 'ethical uprightness' embody an implicit criticism of Smith's own society.[21] By contrast, the future romances of Bellamy, Morris and Wells are more directly engaged with nineteenth-century society and the 'isms and ologies of all descriptions' (*The Crystal Age* 294) which Hudson spurns. For these writers, the future provided a way of 'looking "from the outside" at themselves', and time-travel was used 'to project themselves into the new worlds that were coming into being'.[22] When Edward Bellamy's Julian Guest awakens in the year 2000 (like the hero of Wells's *The Sleeper Awakes*, he has found a too effective cure for his insomnia), he is shown the better society of the future.[23] To begin with, his narrative is addressed to a late-twentieth-century reader, as he tries to explain nineteenth-century society – the class system, unearned income from investments, the combination of 'private luxury' and public squalor that results from 'excessive individualism' (*LB* 58). Then, through a series of dialogues with Dr. Leete, he is told of the more rational system of this future society and how it has developed through the 'process of industrial evolution' (*LB* 67): 'the concentration of capital' (*LB* 71) in the nineteenth century, with its 'tendency toward monopolies' (*LB* 77), finally produced the nation 'organized as one great business corporation' (*LB* 77), 'a monopoly in the profits and economies of which all citizens shared' (*LB* 78). Bellamy's socialist utopia is a form of state capitalism with a highly centralised, bureaucratic organisation and the extension of 'the principle of universal military service' (*LB* 86) to the entire work-force.[24] The final chapters play with the idea of 'the dream': West awakens and finds himself back in nineteenth-century Boston; the narrative of the future appears as a dream which now alienates him from his own society; then West's estranged experience of his own society is revealed to be only a nightmare. These narrative twists, however, produce very little sense of 'hesitation' in the reader, perhaps because of the novel's very firm rational and didactic basis.[25]

News from Nowhere, like *A Crystal Age*, presents a future that resembles the pre-industrial past.[26] Where Bellamy celebrates technological developments, Morris fuses memories of Oxford colleges with quattrocento Italian cities in an idealised dream of the medieval.

Where Bellamy imagines his utopia evolving peacefully out of nineteenth-century conditions, Morris's future-world is the product of class-struggle and cataclysmic change. But Morris resembles Bellamy in that he is less concerned with the 'hesitation' that characterises the fantastic than with didacticism. He makes perfunctory use of falling asleep to effect the time-shift to the future, and his protagonist, like Bellamy's, is merely a teaching aid. 'William Guest' first describes the arrangements in this 'brave new world'; then, through an extended dialogue with the historically-minded 'old Hammond', he learns about the 'systematised robbery' of nineteenth-century economic organisation, the decentralised political and economic organisation of the future, and how the new world was brought into being. Wells's *The Dream* offers an interesting variation on this form of time-travelling: in this case the frame-story is set two thousand years in the future, and the narrator of the inset-story recounts his dream, which is the life-story of Henry Mortimer Smith from his late-Victorian childhood to his death in the 1920s.[27] The status of this dream is, however, somewhat ambiguous: when he first awakes, the narrator observes 'A moment ago I *was* Henry Mortimer Smith', and the dream was so vivid that 'that life' seemed 'the real one' and the present 'only a dream'.[28] As in *Ladies Whose Bright Eyes* and *Connecticut Yankee*, this device produces the effect of parallel universes, but Wells's main interest is in creating a defamiliarised, ironised account of contemporary English social life: Sarnac's narrative of his life as Henry Mortimer Smith is informed by an implicit or explicit comparison with the freer and more rational existence of two thousand years later. In the end, Wells (in *The Dream*), like Bellamy, Hudson and Morris, uses time-travel to produce a teleological narrative, in which the future authorises particular activities in the present. All four romances work with the assertions and absolutes of didactic literature, whereas *Ladies Whose Bright Eyes* takes off from the contradictions of *A Connecticut Yankee* to float free on the uncertainties and hesitations of the fantastic.

III

The defamiliarisation that is produced by juxtaposing different historical periods in these time-travelling narratives is produced in another set of works by the device of the 'wonderful visitor'. Wells's *The Wonderful Visit* epitomises this sub-genre.[29] The 'Strange Bird' seen over Sidderford proves to be an angel, who has somehow slipped into what he thinks of as 'the Land of Dreams'. His wonder at this 'topsy-turvey' (*WV* 24) dream-world of 'mythical monsters' (cows) and 'those Unicorn things ... without horns' (horses) (*WV* 21) leads the Reverend Hillyer to speculate about the 'Four Dimensions' (*WV* 26) and the possibility of 'two worlds' (*WV* 24) – indeed, of numberless parallel universes. The interpretative hypotheses of Morgan and Sorrell are reproduced in this different fantasy: the Angel, for a long time, believes he is dreaming and looks forward to waking up; Dr Crump, who is called in to tend his injury, decides the Angel is 'a mattoid' (*WV* 58), a degenerate who has 'slipped away from confinement' (*WV* 59).[30] Generally, however, the Angel's incomprehension acts as an estranging device – as in his reactions to the 'ugliness' (*WV* 46) of Victorian dress and the uncomfortableness of Victorian furnishings; as in his scandalous inability to understand class; or as when he prompts the Vicar's brief, defamiliarised account of human life (*WV* 78-9). Human incomprehension of the Angel, on the other hand, is used to reveal a matter-of-fact resistance to the wonderful, a rigid adherence to preconceptions – as in the doctor's response to the Angel's 'abnormal growth', the 'reduplication of the anterior limb' with 'simulation of feathers' (*WV* 51), which he offers to remove surgically – and an oppressively narrow conception of human possibilities.

Ford's *Mr Apollo* is clearly derived from Wells's *The Wonderful Visit*.[31] Both works begin with the social comedy produced by the arrival of the supernatural into a materialistic nineteenth-century culture: 'Mr Apollo', like 'Mr Angel', is conducted through a series of encounters which juxtapose the familiar social reality and the transcendent. Mr Apollo experiences the arrest and the court case with which the Angel is threatened, and Apollo, like the Angel, finds it very difficult to convince anyone of his true identity. Beyond this, however, the two works diverge. *Mr Apollo* is less concerned with producing a defamiliarized representation of social reality than with enacting a debate: the conflict between scientific and visionary modes, implicit in *The Wonderful Visit*, is foregrounded and thematized. At the same time, *Mr Apollo* has other concerns and antecedents. At the end of *The Wonderful Visit*, the Angel observes that he 'thought there was nothing beautiful at all in life' (*WV* 222), but then he remembers the Vicar's 'care' for him. In *Mr Apollo*, the importance of 'care' and hospitality is given structural emphasis by reference to the story of Philemon and Baucis, which presents generosity as a moral imperative. (In *Ancient Lights*, Ford notes that 'high ideals were always being held' before him: 'My grandfather ... was not only perpetually giving, he was perpetually enjoining upon all others the necessity of giving never-endingly', *AL* xi-xii.) Alfred and Frances Milne, like Philemon and Baucis, entertain a disguised god and are rewarded by being made his priests. Snitow is very critical of this 'happy ending': 'The Milnes' fate, to be Apollo's priests, can hardly capture our imaginations after we have experienced the rich texture of their personalities'.[32] However, Snitow misses another way in which this ending is problematic: the reward of fresh air, which Apollo brings the ailing Alfred Milne, is produced by the instantaneous demolition of the block of flats outside his window, presumably involving considerable loss of life. Where Wells emphasises the division between the familiar and the transcendent, Ford's fable intimates the dangers of entertaining the divine.[33] In contrast to Wells's lost angel, Ford's Apollo is a powerful and fearful being. The uneasiness of the conclusion is, then, of a piece with the open-ended discussions which constitute so much of Ford's narrative.

Ford's earlier novel, *The Inheritors*, nominally a collaboration with Conrad, shows how closely related the devices of time travel and the wonderful visitor are.[34] 'Miss Etchingham Granger', the Fourth Dimensionist, resembles a traveller from the future. Like Twain's Connecticut Yankee, she is characterised by her superior knowledge and skills: when she explains herself to Granger, he feels it is like 'an enlightened person' talking to 'stupid children', and he complains that she views him as 'relatively a Choctaw' (*Inheritors* 8, 9). Ford's fable, however, derives her from a parallel world, 'an inhabited plain – invisible to our eyes, but omnipresent' (*Inheritors* 9). Like other wonderful visitors, she has difficulty persuading her hosts of her true identity: Granger insists on seeing her as 'a foreigner' or as someone travelling 'incognito' (*Inheritors* 7, 8), just as the Reverend Todd insists on seeing 'Mr Apollo' as foreign royalty travelling incognito. Like other wonderful visitors, too, she is experienced ambiguously by her hosts. In the opening chapters, she seems to Granger both 'regal' and 'devilish' (*Inheritors* 12, 11); by the end, he is forced to see that this fascinating woman has corrupted him. She represents both the replacement of one generation by the next, and the replacement of one culture by another. Granger sees her as 'a type of those who are to inherit the earth' (*Inheritors* 16), but these inheritors are not marked for their meekness; rather they are 'clear-sighted, eminently practical ... with no ideals, prejudices or remorse; with no feeling for art and no reverence for life' (*Inheritors* 9). Like *The Fifth Queen* (or, indeed, the work on Cromwell on which Granger is collaborating with Churchill), *The Inheritors* deals with what it takes to be a turning-point in history: in this case, the replacement of the 'probity' and 'altruism' of old-style Toryism by the new Toryism of Joseph Chamberlain, and the replacement of 'old-fashioned small enterprises' by ruthless individualism and the 'gigantic trusts' (*Inheritors* 169) of monopoly capitalism.[35]

Once freed from the distractions of its relation to *Heart of Darkness* (with Africa unconvincingly replaced by Greenland) and its elements of *roman à clef*, *The Inheritors* emerges as a clearly constructed narrative of political and financial intrigue.[36] It anticipates Conrad's *The Arrow of Gold*, in which a naive young man, through his love for a mysterious young woman, is drawn into a world of political intrigue. It anticipates also *The Fifth Queen*, where Katharine Howard is another innocent who finds herself surrounded by political scheming beyond her comprehension. However, where Katharine sets herself to understand and intervene in the political process, Granger does not want to understand the world that surrounds him. The political process that is gradually revealed in *The Inheritors* is that described by Sarnac in *The Dream*, in his brief history of Victorian England: the landowners 'made a losing fight for predominance against the new industrialists', but these, in turn, 'gave way to a rather different type who developed advertisement and a political and financial use of newspapers and new methods of finance' (*D* 317). Granger's literary career is caught up in these changes: he begins as an unsuccessful writer with high literary ideals; he is persuaded by the popular author Callan to produce a series of articles, 'Atmospheres' (somewhat like the pieces Willa Cather produced for *McClure's Magazine* or the 'Literary Portraits' that Ford was later to supply to the *Daily Mail* and the *Tribune*); and he exposes to our gaze the publishing world of Polehampton and Lea, in which a manuscript can be rejected because it is 'too good to be marketable' (*Inheritors* 49). Ford, however, is not just up-dating Gissing's *New Grub Street*: he is concerned with more than the corruption of literary standards through the encounter with the market-place. He demonstrates the compromises and corruption involved in the new political and financial power of the press: Granger finds himself obliged to write a flattering piece on the Duc de Mersch, who is one of the journal's financial backers; Callan similarly finds himself called upon to produce a report on Mersch's 'System for the Regeneration of the Arctic Regions'. The narrative pivots on the imperialism which invalidates the 'conscious rectitude gang' (*Inheritors* 204) of the old order, but it foregrounds the nature of the new order that is replacing it.

The sense of an old order passing is economically suggested by Granger's position as the last male of an 'old family': there have been 'Grangers of Etchingham', Granger asserts, 'since the flood' (*Inheritors* 28), and Granger is conscious of having 'family traditions and graves' (*Inheritors* 112) behind him. This is supported by the character of Granger's aunt, 'a great dowager landowner' (*Inheritors* 55), and by her political salon in Paris, a *Salon des Causes Perdues* (*Inheritors* 82) like the Delestang *salon* Conrad visited in Marseilles, in which various Legitimists offer a subtle parallel to the doomed political world of whose passing Granger has been given advance notice.[37] Miss Granger has 'the pathos attaching to the last of a race, of a type; the air of waiting for the deluge' (*Inheritors* 132), while the nostalgia of the Legitimists for pre-Revolutionary France further promotes the Revolution as a subject-rhyme for the political shift marked by the events of the novel. Miss Granger's final physical collapse marks the end of an era as clearly as the cutting down of Groby Great Tree does in *Parade's End*.

At the novel's climax, Granger is faced with a decision: he can save the old order by suppressing Callan's report on the Duc de Mersch's operation in Greenland or he can let the report be published and bring down everything he holds dear. As he realises, the 'old order of things' had 'to live or perish with a lie' (*Inheritors* 185). He faces a similar choice to Marlow when confronted by Kurtz's Intended. Unlike Marlow, he chooses to publish the truth rather than maintain the 'old order of things' with a lie; but the decision is no more straightforward than Marlow's. The reader's attitude to Granger has been unstable throughout the narrative: now, rather than producing a moral resolution, Granger's decision is immediately opened to questions. While he presents it to himself as staying loyal to his pseudo-sister (as Marlow tries to stay loyal to Kurtz and M. George to Dona Rita), she dispassionately emphasises that he has proved 'false' to his standards 'at a supreme moment' (*Inheritors* 210) and betrayed himself and others for purely selfish reasons. Throughout the novel, Granger has wished to maintain a sense of himself as 'clean-handed in the matter' (*Inheritors* 57), but he is finally forced to recognise that he has been 'scratching the backs of all sorts of creatures'. At the close, he is made to look at the historical and political processes he had hoped to ignore, and his sense of himself as a free agent, making moral decisions, is confronted by the idea that his individuality has merely been part of 'an immense machine – unconcerned, soulless, but all its parts made up of bodies of men' (*Inheritors* 206).

IV

In these various fantasies of time-travellers, dreamers and wonderful visitors, there are two recurrent features. In the first place, a number of these fantasies are very firmly rooted in specific geographical locations. *Ladies Whose Bright Eyes* begins on a train travelling from Southampton to London; most of the action takes place on Salisbury Plain; and the final chapter moves from Sorrell's publishing offices in Covent Garden back to Salisbury.[38] *News from Nowhere* very precisely maps its future world against nineteenth-century London. William Guest's first glimpse of the Thames near Hammersmith explicitly makes the comparison:

> The soap-works with their smoke-vomiting chimneys were gone; the engineer's works gone; the lead-works gone; and no sound of riveting and hammering came down the west wind from Thorneycroft's. (*NN* 7)

Elsewhere, the comparison is often implicit, as in the description of the woodlands extending from Kensington 'northward and west right over Paddington and a little way down Notting Hill', then 'north-east to Primrose Hill, and so on': 'rather a narrow strip of it gets through Kingsland to Stoke-Newington and Clapton, where it spreads out along the heights above the Lea Marshes' (*NN* 29). In *The Dream*, Sarnac's account of Harry Mortimer Smith's life in Victorian England reproduces one of the *topoi* of Victorian evocations of London: 'a vast traffic of clumsy automobiles and distressed horses in narrow unsuitable streets ... a nightmare of multitudes, a suffocating realisation of jostling discomfort and uncleanness and of an unedurable strain on eye and ear and attention'.[39] This is the prelude to a very careful physical and sociological mapping of Smith's life in London from his first residence in Pimlico's 'great wilderness of streets of dingy grey houses in which people lived and let lodgings', through walks along the Embankment to St Paul's, or from Regent Street and Piccadilly through Cheapside to Clerkenwell, to his observations of the 'nocturnal promenade under the electric lamps' of Wilton Street and Victoria Street and his pleasure trips to Richmond, Kew and Hampton Court.

The other recurrent feature of these works is a self-conscious reproduction of the conditions of their own production. As we have seen, one of the narrative concerns of *The Inheritors* is how Granger, 'a writer with high – with the highest – ideals' (*Inheritors* 5), clearly a version of Ford himself, is brought into the literary market place. Through Callan he is persuaded to undertake a 'series of studies of celebrities' for the Northcliffean Fox's new paper:

> 'It will be a new line, or rather – what is a great deal better, mind you – an old line treated in a slightly, very slightly different way. That's what the public wants.' (*Inheritors* 21)

Callan stands as a warning of what Granger might become: like Granger, he 'had ideals in his youth and had starved a little' (*Inheritors* 24), but he has set himself to supply 'what the public wants', and his new novel prompts Granger to the horrified thought 'I, too, must cynically offer this sort of stuff if I was ever to sell my tens of thousands' (*Inheritors* 24). The representation of the literary market-place is completed by the portrait of the publisher T. Fisher Unwin as Polehampton – a man, uneasy with books and shamelessly penny-pinching with his authors, for whom publishing is a means to financial and political success.[40] He is contrasted to his reader, Lea, a sympathetic portrait of Edward Garnett (who had been dismissed by Unwin at the end of 1899). Lea is Granger's literary conscience: 'Lea, you see, stood for what was best in the mode of thought that I was casting aside. He stood for the aspiration' (*Inheritors* 48). In *Ladies Whose Bright Eyes*, the narrative is framed by accounts of Sorrell's work as a publisher.[41] The opening chapter repeats Ford's complaint about the changing priorities of publishing. Sorrell reflects:

In the old days a publisher had to consider what was Literature.... Now it was just a business. You found out what the public had to have and gave it them. (*LWBE* 11)

Sorrell, however, welcomes this change. He has modified 'the old-fashioned publishing traditions' of the family firm in the direction of supplying 'what the city clerk would want' (*LWBE 13*):

...books, if you got hold of the right sort of books, were something that the city clerk must have. The right sort of book was as indispensable as a season ticket, a clean collar, or a radio set. (*LWBE* 12)

Consequently, he had 'begun with encyclopaedias', then 'cheap editions of the classics originally published by Sorrell and Sons' (*LWBE* 13), and he is now returning from buying the English rights to a book about a flight around the earth: the aviator 'had written a book about his intrepid exploit – or had had it written for him so that it had been awaiting him when he got back to New York' (*LWBE* 9-10). In the final chapter, the success of this book and discussions about Bunter's regular volumes of salacious memoirs form the context for Sorrell's decision to give up publishing:

'His "Love affairs of Ninon de l'Enclos" had done six thousand. This one would do forty. He would give them medieval love.' (*LWBE* 344)

Bunter's account of 'medieval love' clearly stands in sharp contrast to Sorrell's love for Dionissia.

The Dream provides a more complex and analytic account of the changes in publishing in this period. Sarnac begins by recounting the inadequate educational provisions made for the 'accumulating masses of the population' by the 'learned and prosperous classes': the 'ill-equipped and under-staffed schoolhouses', the interminable hours of learning facts by rote, the whole process 'truncated by employment at thirteen or fourteen, when curiosity and interest were just beginning to awaken', produced 'a vast multitude of people, just able to read, credulous and uncritical and pitifully curious to learn about life and things'. In other words, Forster's 1871 Education Act, which at last legislated for universal elementary education, created the readership which Newnes identified and catered for with *Tit-Bits*. As Sarnac tells it:

> ... legend related that one day after reading aloud some item of interest to his family he remarked, 'I call that a regular titbit'. From that feat of nomenclature he went on to the idea of a weekly periodical full of scraps of interest, cuttings from books and newspapers and the like. A hungry multitude, eager and curious, was ready to feed greedily on such *hors d'oeuvres*.

And, 'hard upon the heels of Newnes', came Arthur Pearson and the Harmsworth brothers, publishing 'a shoal of novelette magazines and cheap domestic newspapers for women, young girls and children', scientific handbooks and guides of various sorts. According to Sarnac, the result was that 'there were practically two educational worlds and two traditions of intellectual culture side by side':

> 'There was ... the new publishing, the new press, the cinema-theatres and so forth, a crude mental uproar arising out of the new elementary schools of the nineteenth century, and there was the old aristocratic education of the seventeenth and eighteenth centuries, which had picked up its tradition from the Augustan Age of Rome.'

Wells's reading of this situation, however, is quite different from Ford's. Sarnac goes on to compare the products of the new order, who have 'the intellectual courage and vigour ... of Aristotle and Plato', with the 'pseudo-educated man of the older order', who has the mentality of 'the household-slave': 'the same abject respect for patron, prince and patrician ... the same meticulous care in minor matters ... the same fear of uncharted reality'.

Wells's earlier work, *The Sea-Lady*, is much closer to Ford's attitude.[42] Like *Mr Apollo*, it contains a certain amount of satire on the popular press. In 'a brilliant stroke of modern journalism', the *New York*

Yell invents the story of a 'pure American girl' that Charteris has 'jilted' (*S-L* 115, 114). In the same way, the English newspaper editor is not interested in the facts about 'the Sea Lady':

> '... the public ... buys our paper to swallow it, and it's got to go down easy ... I thought you was on to a mixed bathing scandal or something of that sort – with Juice in it.' (*S-L* 80-81)

It touches, with similar lightness, on developments in publishing. Charteris, for example, is described as being employed in 'the Higher Journalism'; in addition, 'he wrote some very passable verse, and edited Jane Austen for the only publisher who had not already reprinted the works of that classic lady' (*S-L* 112, 113). The fullest treatment of contemporary publishing, however, comes in the Sea Lady's account of the 'Deep Sea Reading' of the mermaids and mermen, who, she argues, 'form indeed a distinct reading public' (*S-L* 33). They have been able to get hold of 'practically the whole of the Tauchnitz Library', dropped from the careless hands of travellers into the English channel as well as 'American reprints in the Mersey' (*S-L* 35). They have also had the benefit of 'the Deep Sea Mission for Fishermen ... raining down tracts' (*S-L* 35) and 'the *Times* reprint of the Encyclopaedia Britannica' (*S-L* 38) not to mention Richard Garnett's 'All-Literature Sausage' designed so that 'almost any businessman may take hold of everything in literature now practically without hindrance to his more serious occupations' (*S-L* 38). The novel begins as a serio-comic combination of *Undine* and *Madame Bovary*. The narrator observes that 'it must have been from the common latter-day novel and the newspaper that the Sea Lady derived her ideas of human life and sentiment' (*S-L* 40). Certainly, she presents herself, at times, as a burlesque of the social problem novel, as when she asserts that she 'never had a mother' and has no 'right to a surname' (*S-L* 46). Subsequently, the novel engages with that other important component of Victorian fantasy, when the Sea Lady seeks to persuade that human life is 'a dream' and 'there are better dreams' (*S-L* 159,160): 'there was another existence, an Elsewhere' (*S-L* 173). As Melville says, she whispers that 'this life is a phantom life, unreal, flimsy, limited' (*S-L* 239); at the same time, she is 'something that stands for things unseen ... Something we never find in life ... Something we are always seeking' (*S-L* 242). She thus produces that sense of alternate realities found in other stories of 'wonderful visitors', and, in particular, she articulates that opposition between 'the sensible' (*S-L* 168) and the transcendent that Ford engages with in *Mr Apollo*. In the end, however, it is another kind of opposition upon which the narrative comes to focus. In her relationship with Charteris, she seems to represent both desire and death, and the narrative hesitates between the two readings. Indeed, the final words of the novel resemble the inconclusiveness of Marlow at the end of *Lord Jim*. After Charteris departs, 'hastening downward out of this life of ours to unknown and inconceivable things' (*S-L* 297), the narrative concludes:

> And of the end I can only guess and dream. Did there come a sudden horror upon him at the last, a sudden perception of infinite error, and was he drawn down, swiftly and terribly, a bubbling repentance into those unknown depths? Or was she tender and wonderful to the last, and did she wrap her arms about him and draw him down, down until the soft waters closed above him, down into a gentle ecstasy of death? (*S-L* 299)

In this work, then, Wells approaches a quality that generally distinguishes Ford's fantasies from the others I have discussed. As Snitow has argued, most of these fantasists 'were ultimately defenders of some kind of spiritual and mental certainty' (121), whereas, for Ford, 'the link between the mind and the world was tenuous, dangerous, misleading and mysterious' (120). As a result, his works generate 'a bottomless succession of unresolved attitudes' (2).[43] Ford in *The Inheritors*, *Mr Apollo* and *Ladies Whose Bright Eyes* takes over some of the figures and devices of Edwardian fantasy, but he uses them to produce a fiction of unresolved contradictions, a fiction of modernist open-endedness.

ROBERT HAMPSON

NOTES

1. Tzvetan Todorov, *The Fantastic: A Structural Approach to a Literary Genre*, tr. R. Howard, Cleveland, Ohio: Case Western Reserve University Press; Ithaca, N.Y.: Cornell University Press, 1973, 1975, p. 33. Kathryn Hume, in *Fantasy and Mimesis*, London: Methuen, 1984, offers a critique of Todorov's attempt to treat fantasy as a genre (pp. 13-28). She also supplies a taxonomy of recent definitions of fantasy and emphasises the problematic nature of the term. Her working definition, 'fantasy is any departure from consensus reality' (p. 21) has been adopted in selecting works for consideration in this essay.

2. *Ladies Whose Bright Eyes* was first published in London by Constable & Co. in 1911. A revised version was published in Philadelphia by J. B. Lippincott in 1935. My discussion refers to the later text.

3. Freud includes 'the flying dream' in the category of 'typical dreams' in *The Interpretation of Dreams*. He records Strümpell's somatic reading of such dreams: 'the flying dream is the image which is found appropriate by the mind as an interpretation of the stimulus produced by the rising and sinking of the lobes of the lungs at times when cutaneous sensations in the thorax have ceased to be conscious' (*The Interpretation of Dreams*, Pelican Freud Library, vol. 4, Harmondsworth, 1980, p. 101; L. Strümpell, *Die Natur und Entstehung der Träume*, Leipzig, 1887). Freud also offers his own interpretation in terms of 'the masturbatory desires of the pubertal period' (p. 507).

4. In revising the novel for the 1935 edition, Ford moved the original Chapter 5 – it became the new Chapter 3 – to produce this effect.

5. Compare James Cameron's *Terminator* (1984) and Stephen Spielberg's *Back to the Future* (1984), both of which foreground the oedipal possibilities of time-travel. In *Back to the Future*, McFly's mother falls in love with her time-travelling son – and the son has to encourage his father's wooing in order to bring about his own existence; in *Terminator*, the son 'gives birth' to the father by the process of time-travel, having already programmed the father's involvement with the mother, to bring about his own birth. *Terminator*, indeed, constructs a version of the Christian birth-story (complete with annunciation and slaughter of the innocents): Sarah Connors is told that she will bear the child who will save humanity, but, in this version, it is the Son who sends the Father, and the Father who sacrifices his life. Compare also Francis Ford Coppola's *Peggy Sue Got Married* (1986).

52

6. Henry Adams, *The Education of Henry Adams,* Boston and New York: Houghton Mifflin, 1918, pp. 228-9.

7. Compare Kathryn Hume's account of 'contrastive literature' which 'forces us to try to make sense out of two clashing views of reality' (p. 94).

8. He might also have been conscious of William Morris's 'Lindenberg Pool', first published in the *Oxford and Cambridge Magazine* (1856), in which the narrator suddenly discovers he is no longer in the nineteenth century but has become a thirteenth-century priest. See *The Early Romances of William Morris,* London: Dent, 1907.

9. In his essay, 'The Two Sorrells of Ford Madox Ford', *Modern Philology,* 59 (November 1961), pp. 114-21, which contains a detailed account of the changes between the two editions, Richard Cassell sums up the different endings as follows: 'The 1935 version is a challenge to society. Instead of an escape, it offers a confrontation'. The 1911 version anticipates Ford's own post-war, rural retreat with Stella Bowen, whereas the 1935 version (which was written in New York in the early 1930s) has to be seen in the context of the excitement at the prospect of a new era and new social order that was prevalent on the American left at this time. In Louis Zukofsky's great poem *A,* for example, *A*-8 suggests that the decline of the Adams family in America 'comes to its conclusion just as another cycle of growth begins in Russia' and Lenin and Stalin are seen as 'new Adamses' living 'in the right time and place' (Barry Ahearn, 'The Adams Connection', in Carroll F. Terrell, *Louis Zukofsky: Man and Poet,* Orono, Maine: The National Poetry Foundation, 1979, p. 124). See Daniel Aaron, *Writers on the Left* and Eric Homberger, *American Writers and Radical Politics 1900-39,* London: Macmillan, 1988.

10. Mark Twain, *A Connecticut Yankee at King Arthur's Court* (1889) Harmondsworth: Penguin Classics, 1986, p. 33; hereafter cited in the text as *CY.* Ford has also reproduced many of the unresolved contradictions of Twain's work. For an account of these contradictions, see Darko Suvin, *Metamorphoses of Science Fiction,* New Haven: Yale University Press, 1979, pp. 193-202.

11. Rider Haggard, *King Solomon's Mines,* London: Cassell & Co., 1885.

12. Hume observes, 'The Boss's tyranny was merely more effectively tyrannical than that which it replaced' (p. 140). There is an obvious similarity to the development of the Gould Concession in relation to the people of Costaguana in *Nostromo.*

13. See Henry Nash Smith, *Mark Twain's Fable of Progress: Political and Economic Ideas in 'A Connecticut Yankee',* New Brunswick, N.J.: Rutgers University Press, 1964.

14. To further the latter aspect of Morgan, Twain draws on the pre-Revolutionary position of the French aristocracy and on slave-owning in America for his construction of 'sixth-century England'.

15. As Smith demonstrates, although 'the businessman is the moral norm invoked' (p. 75) by Twain's satire in the campaign against chivalry, the novel proves to be ambivalent: what at times seems a fable advocating technology and capitalism can also be read as the opposite. Hume comments on the ambiguity of the alignment of technology and war: 'When Twain undercuts the world of technology so drastically, we are left to try to untangle what values he really does expect us to draw from the story' (p. 140).

16. *The Fantastic*, p. 169.

17. Stephen Prickett, *Victorian Fantasy*, Hassocks, Sussex: Harvester, 1979. As Prickett intimates, the popularity of the *Arabian Nights* was also a factor. For a fuller exploration of this area, see Peter Caracciolo (ed.), *The 'Arabian Nights' in English Literature*, Basingstoke: Macmillan, 1988.

18. Charles Kingsley, *The Water Babies*, London, 1863; Lewis Carroll, *Alice in Wonderland*, London, 1865, and *Through the Looking-glass*, London: Macmillan, 1872; George MacDonald, *Lilith: a romance*, London: Chatto & Windus, 1895. As Prickett notes, Coleridge added an epigraph to 'The Ancient Mariner' affirming his belief in the importance of contemplating 'the image of a larger and better world' lest the mind 'habituated to the small concerns of daily life, limit itself too much', and the numerous nineteenth-century illustrations of the poem picked up 'the tension between apparent irrationality and hidden meaning', which is used to imply 'the existence of "other worlds", mysterious and yet almost familiar, lying just beyond the frontiers of our normal world' (p. 34).

19. W. H. Hudson, *A Crystal Age*, London: Duckworth, 1906, v. Compare Hume, who ascribes the impulse to fantasy to a desire to change reality 'out of boredom, play, vision, longing for something lacking' (p. 20). See also Darko Suvin, *Victorian Science Fiction in the U. K.: the Discourses of Knowledge and of Power*, Boston: G. K. Hall, 1983, on the pre-occupation with the future as a sign of lack and on the sudden increased publication of future fantasies after 1871 (pp. 388-9).

20. Ruth Tomalin, *W. H. Hudson: A Biography*, London: Faber, 1982, p. 133.

21. David Miller, *W. H. Hudson and the Elusive Paradise*, Basingstoke: Macmillan, 1990, p. 119.

22. William Bellamy, *The Novels of Wells, Bennett and Galsworthy: 1890-1910*

London: Routledge & Kegan Paul, 1971, p. 22; Snitow, p. 107.

23. Edward Bellamy, *Looking Backward*, Boston: Ticknor & Co., 1888; hereafter cited in the text as *LB*.

24. For a fuller analysis of *Looking Backward*, see A. L. Morton, *The English Utopia*, London: Lawrence & Wishart, 1952, pp. 193-98, and Suvin, *Metamorphoses*, pp. 171-78.

25. Contrast *Lilith* and *The Water Babies*. *Lilith* generates a hesitation about which 'world' is real and which is dream; in *The Water Babies*, Tom's magical escape from reality discovers a world which gradually seems more real and substantial than nineteenth-century English society.

26. First printed in *The Commonweal*, 1890, and, in book form by Roberts Brothers, Boston, 1890, *News from Nowhere* was written as a reply to *Looking Backward*. For a fuller account, see Suvin, *Metamorphoses*, pp. 178-92. Suvin argues that *News from Nowhere* is 'not to be taken for positivist prophecy but for the figure or type of a fulfillment that could or should come' (p. 184). All references are to the Pocket Library Edition, London: Longmans, Green, 1914, hereafter cited in the text as *NN*.

27. H. G. Wells, *The Dream*, London: Jonathan Cape, 1924; hereafter cited in the text as *D*.

28. Wells's model is probably the tale 'The Two Lives of Sultan Mahmoud', which tells how Sultan Mahmoud lives a whole lifetime in the seconds that pass between immersing his head in a bowl of water and re-surfacing again. This first appeared in English in 'The History of Chec Chahabeddin' in *Turkish Tales* (1708); it was included in the J. C. Mardrus edition of the *Arabian Nights* (1899-1904).

29. H. G. Wells, *The Wonderful Visit*, London: Dent, 1895; hereafter cited in the text as *WV*.

30. As the language suggests, Crump is a disciple of Nordau and Lombroso. Lombroso's concept of the 'mattoid' underlies Conrad's conception of Winnie in *The Secret Agent* (which was dedicated to Wells). See R. G. Hampson, '"If you read Lombroso": Conrad and Criminal Anthropology', in Mario Curreli (ed.), *The Ugo Mursia Memorial Lectures*, Milan: Mursia International, 1987, pp. 317-35.

31. Early reviews compared it unfavourably with Wells's work: the reviewer in the *Saturday Review* argued that *Mr Apollo* was a failure because it lacked 'that lightness and humour which made so much more acceptable the fashion in which Mr Wells once dealt

with a celestial visitor' (*Saturday Review*, 106 [5 September 1908], 304); the reviewer in the *Athenaeum* observed that 'while Mr Wells employs a genial humour and a strong imagination, Mr Hueffer shows only irony and fancy' (*Athenaeum*, 4220 [12 September 1908], p. 297).

32. Snitow, p. 118.

33. It is possible that Ford also had in mind either Molière's or Kleist's *Amphitryon*, which tells how Jupiter visits Alkmene disguised as her husband, makes her pregnant and creates all kinds of problems for her.

34. *The Inheritors: An Extravagant Story* (1901), London: Dent, 1923; hereafter cited in the text as *Inheritors*. Conrad wrote in Thomas J. Wise's copy, 'The idea of this book is entirely Hueffer's, and so is most of the writing'. See Jocelyn Baines, *Joseph Conrad: A Critical Biography* (1960), Harmondsworth: Pelican Books, 1971, p. 292.

35. Arthur Mee's *Joseph Chamberlain: A Romance of Modern Politics*, London: S.W. Partridge, 1901, suggests something of how Chamberlain was regarded at this time. The book begins by saying that 'No other man so sharply divides the opinion of the nation' and makes the ominous observation that 'the time has never been when the honour and character of our public men were of more account in the world than now' (Prefatory Note). After hints about Chamberlain's possible collusion with the 'Jameson Raid', Mee ends by describing him as 'a man to whom the British Empire is a limitless field for buying and selling' (p. 141); by alluding to the 'debate on his connections with companies contracting with the Government' (p. 151); and by a coded reference to the need for 'sacrifice' ('he has not readily responded to the call for sacrifice which comes to all public men in the interest of public honour and public credit', p. 151).

36. The choice of Greenland to replace Africa was probably influenced by Conrad's interest in F. L. McClintock's *The Voyage of the 'Fox' in the Arctic Seas*, London: John Murray, 1859, which refers to the Royal Danish Greenland Company and reflects favourably on how much the Danish Government has done for the inhabitants of Greenland.

37. This *salon* appears again in *The Arrow of Gold*.

38. Moser suggests that Sorrell's disorientation on Salisbury Plain draws on Ford's own experience there in July 1904, when (according to Olive Garnett) he became 'practically a wandering lunatic' (Moser, p. 84).

39. See R. G. Hampson, '"Topographical Mysteries": Conrad and London', in Gene M. Moore (ed.), *Conrad's Cities: Essays for Hans van Marle*, Amsterdam / Atlanta, GA.:

1992, pp. 159-74.

40. Cedric Watts, in *Joseph Conrad: A Literary Life*, Basingstoke: Macmillan, 1989, observes that T. Fisher Unwin has 'received a rather bad press over the years as a cold, calculating, tightfisted publisher' (p. 52). He notes, in Fisher Unwin's favour, that, when Chesson and Garnett saw merit in the manuscript of Conrad's first novel, 'he acted without demur on Chesson's recommendation, met the author personally, encouraged him to maintain his literary ambitions, provided exceptional publicity, and entered into a detailed postal discussion of Conrad's future works' (p. 52).

41. In *A Connecticut Yankee*, Morgan had set himself up as a newspaper owner and had introduced into Arthurian England the ethos of the American newspaper world of the 1880s (and after) complete with publicity stunts. See Christopher P. Wilson, *The Labor of Words: Literary Professionalism in the Progressive Era*, Athens, Ga.: University of Georgia Press, 1985, and J. H. Wiener (ed.), *Papers for the Millions: The New Journalism in Britain, 1850s to 1914*, New York: Greenwood, 1988.

42. H. G. Wells, *The Sea-Lady: A Tissue of Moonshine*, London: Methuen, 1902; hereafter cited in the text as *S-L*.

43. See, however, John Huntington, *The Logic of Fantasy: H. G. Wells and Science Fiction*, N.Y.: Columbia University Press, 1982, for a reading of Wells's early fiction as unstable, self-subverting, and open-ended.

FORD AND PRE-RAPHAELITISM

Pamela Bickley

I take nothing back; what I have written is the exact truth. And yet ...
(*AL* 289)

Ford began his literary career as a serious reviewer of Pre-Raphaelitism, eager to emphasise his family connections with Pre-Raphaelite artists and writers. His early poetry is inspired by Pre-Raphaelite subjects and frequently echoes Pre-Raphaelite verse. Similarly, stylistic devices and thematic predilections generally identified as Pre-Raphaelite can be detected in a number of his early novels. However, from about 1910 Ford can be seen to commence a series of complex manoeuvres in which he variously rejects or defends Pre-Raphaelitism, while simultaneously retaining his role as a Pre-Raphaelite authority.

I. Ford's Pre-Raphaelite Identity

Ford's critical writings on the Pre-Raphaelites fall into two principal categories: reviews and book-length studies. In the 1890s and the first decade of the twentieth century, Ford was one of the chief reviewers of Pre-Raphaelitism. Posthumous exhibitions and the publication of memoirs and obituaries meant that Pre-Raphaelitism was still subject to serious assessment at this time. Ford supplied the introductory notes to exhibitions of Ford Madox Brown's work in 1896 and 1909; he reviewed exhibitions of work by Millais and Rossetti in 1896 – as well as William Michael Rossetti's edition of Rossetti's *Family Letters*; he wrote obituaries on the deaths of Burne-Jones (1898) and Holman Hunt (1910); and, finally, he returned to both Christina and D. G. Rossetti in full-length articles in 1911. In all of these writings, Ford presupposes the significance of Pre-Raphaelitism. While he deplores the affectations of *fin-de-siècle* aestheticism, he consistently asserts that the Pre-Raphaelites were authentically revolutionary spirits who 'cleared away from a whole side of human life a mass of hideous shams and

PAMELA BICKLEY

conventions'.[1] At the same time, Ford's chief objection to Pre-Raphaelite art is always that it fails to engage successfully with the contemporary world:

> [Burne-Jones] gives his life to the search for beauty, and he seemed to find it in every age, but never in the hours that were passing.[2]

By contrast, his own aim, as he put it in the Preface to his *Collected Poems*, was 'to register my own times in terms of my own time' (*CP1* 13).

Ford's major studies of Pre-Raphaelitism are *Ford Madox Brown: A Record of His Life and Work* (1896); *Rossetti: A Critical Essay on His Art* (1902); and *The Pre-Raphaelite Brotherhood: A Critical Monograph* (1907). In his study of Ford Madox Brown, Ford spends some time analysing the Pre-Raphaelite cultivation of an intense particularity of detail. As Ann Barr Snitow observes, Ford's own work shares this Pre-Raphaelite fixation on detail.[3] However, his main purpose in this book is to chart the achievement of his grandfather – and assist in the process of mythologising the artist.[4] In *Rossetti*, Ford inherits his father's interest.[5] Here, too, the artist emerges as an heroic figure: Ford, for example, approves Rossetti's 'constitutional contempt for maxims of authority' (*Rossetti* 16). Nevertheless, for Ford, Rossetti remains an 'Amateur in two arts'. In painting, which is the principal object of Ford's analysis, Rossetti's success is limited by inadequacies of technique and his growing adherence to literary and symbolic subject matter. *The Pre-Raphaelite Brotherhood* restricts itself to an account of the earliest years of the Brotherhood (1848-1853).[6] Ford describes the initiating aims and inspiration of the Brotherhood and clarifies the distinctions between early Pre-Raphaelite art and its later sub-divisions into mid-century genre painting – 'a sort of innocuous daily bread' – and the literary, medieval art of Rossetti, Morris, and Burne-Jones which became 'Aestheticist'.[7] At the same time, Ford formulates his sense of 'the danger of the Literary Ideal' and expresses his distaste, in particular,

60

for the didacticism inherent in Hunt's 'superstition that the moral idea is necessary to a rendering of life' (*PRB* 118).

In *Ancient Lights and Certain New Reflections* (1911), Ford changes his emphasis. The 'ancient lights' are the leading lights of Pre-Raphaelitism and aestheticism. However, as Saunders points out, an 'ancient light' is 'a window whose light is legally protected from obstruction by new buildings' (I, 68). The Pre-Raphaelites may be 'admirable monuments', but they also implicitly inhibit new developments (I, 68). Ford defines the Pre-Raphaelite Movement, in its strictest sense, as moribund by 1870, having bequeathed 'a curse that has miasmically affected the English world of letters!' (*AL* 239). He conjures up a perpetually foggy Bloomsbury, where the Pre-Raphaelites 'sang on bravely of Lancelot and Guinevere' (*AL* 37). And Dante Gabriel Rossetti – the subject of a critical but relatively appreciative, full-length study by Ford in 1902 – by 1911 has become a target for sensational anecdote as well as being credited with responsibility for 'the death of English poetry': 'the art of writing in English received the numbing blow of a sand-bag when Rossetti wrote ... the Blessed Damozel' (*AL* 52-3).

It could be expected that, by 1911, Ford would desire to distance himself from the Victorians; he was already editor of the *English Review* and would have defined his own artistic *confrères* as James, Pound, and, above all, Conrad, whom he placed in the role of rescuer: 'But for him I should have been a continuation of DANTE GABRIEL ROSSETTI' (*LF* 127).[8] As Wiley and Kestner have argued, this 'last Pre-Raphaelite' increasingly disavowed his Pre-Raphaelite ancestors in favour of a modernist persona.[9] But Ford is contradictory and inconsistent. He intersperses his mockery with startlingly hyperbolic statements of praise: the P. R. B. in its inception had made 'a mark such as perhaps no body of men has made upon intellectual Anglo-Saxondom since the days of Shakespeare' (*AL* 23). In June 1911, in a substantial (and neglected) essay on Rossetti in *The Bookman*, Ford took issue with the countless 'exceedingly dull ... misleadingly accurate posthumous biographies of Rossetti' (including his own), and proclaimed Rossetti's 'greatness':

> He was great in the exact sense of the word – for greatness in a writer ... implies the power to voice great multitudes ... So that my own private image of Rossetti the writer and the painter is of something a little vague, very romantic and exceedingly great. He seems to sweep his fingers over the harp-strings of innumerable hearts, calling out the music that is in them.[10]

Ford goes on to make extensive personal and national claims for Rossetti. Ford's own intellectual and artistic identity is defined in the light of Rossetti's poetic achievement:

> You have to ask yourself what you would be, what your mental development would have been, how your intimate self would have grown, if that man had never existed. And think of what we should all have been if Rossetti had never existed.

From this it is only a short step to asserting that England, without his influence, would have been 'Prussianised ... Americanised'.[11]

Nowhere is Ford more anxious and contradictory than in his perception of his own place within a Pre-Raphaelite genealogy. There is the bruised and retiring figure of the following recollection:

> I had been too much hammered by the Pre-Raphaelites. So that my troubled mind took refuge in an almost passionate desire for self-effacement. (*TR* 202)

On the other hand, when, in 1935, his daughter Julia had protested 'I *detest* the Pre-Raffaelites' (sic), Ford had countered that her Pre-Raphaelite ancestry would prove an unavoidable and valuable artistic inheritance:

> ... you were speaking to one who passes for the greatest living expert in that particular matter. I am indeed usually called the last of the pre-Raffaelites

and you, if you practise any of the arts ... will inevitably in time inherit that sobriquet. (*LF* 240)

Indeed, the 'poor dear old Pre-Raphaelite Brotherhood' (*TR* 37) makes an unexpected re-appearance in Ford's late critical works. *Mightier than the Sword* (1938) contains 'memories and criticisms' of Turgenev, James, Conrad, Wells ... and Swinburne. In *The March of Literature* (1939), Ford protests that 'we pre-Raphaelites' were not the 'depressed beings that Gilbert and Sullivan ridiculed' (*ML* 773). If Pre-Raphaelite figures appear somewhat incongruous in these late surveys, it is perhaps because Ford is keeping Pre-Raphaelitism alive at a time when, critically, it is least regarded. But he is also re-creating his own heroic artistic past.

Pre-Raphaelitism always formed part of the myth-making of Ford's own life. Both Stella Bowen and Kenneth Rexroth attest to Ford's prodigious enjoyment as an 'incorrigible romancer' who 'could hold a room full of people spell-bound for an evening with the most intimate details of the pre-Raphaelite moral underground'.[12] Ford clearly exploited to the full his role as 'the greatest living expert' on pre-Raphaelitism. However, his authority might, at times, be open to question. Rexroth recalls one anecdote:

> Swinburne sitting on the floor, his scarlet locks enclosed in the celadon green velvet thighs of the Sid seated on a settee in a mullioned bay reading the Marquis de Sade in her nervous consumptive voice and sticking the poet betimes with her embroidery needle while blonde baby Fordie looked on ... (*Buckshee*, xvii)

Whether this is Ford romancing or Rexroth out-Fording Ford, there is no doubt about the impossibility of this scene, given that Elizabeth Siddal died in 1862, and Ford wasn't born until 1873. As Saunders has shown, Ford was continually engaged in re-shaping his autobiography.[13] This is a process of which Ford was conscious and an idea with which he is always pre-occupied:

Renan says that as soon as one writes about oneself one poetises a little. I don't think I do. On the other hand, being a novelist, it is possible that I romance. (*RY* viii)

Ford's oscillations, however, should not be viewed merely as indicative of the changing fashion for Pre-Raphaelitism. Ford is consistent in his rejection of the decadent, enervated aestheticism which succeeded Pre-Raphaelitism. Equally, he invariably defends the members of the original P. R. B. as individuals. In *Ancient Lights*, attempting to define 'Where we Stand', Ford claims that they were 'to a man, rather burly, passionate creatures, extraordinarily romantic, extraordinarily enthusiastic, and most impressively quarrelsome' (*AL* 3). Ford's critical and autobiographical writing on the Pre-Raphaelites is, then, artfully disingenuous. He spends a considerable portion of his writing life inventing the background he desires to reject; yet, in ostensibly denying Pre-Raphaelitism, he actually draws the reader's attention to it. An examination of some of the ways in which Pre-Raphaelitism informs Ford's writing reveals that it can often provide a *point d'appui* either in the form of a specific allusion (the indebtedness of *The 'Half Moon'* to Rossetti's 'Sister Helen', for example) or, as in the case of the Tietjens novels, supplying a comparative framework which illumines Ford's central focus.

II. Ford's Pre-Raphaelite Poetry

In *Return to Yesterday*, Ford referred to the 'powerful shadow of Pre-Raphaelism' (sic) (*RY* 78). Snitow is surely right in her assessment that, if the young Ford experienced 'a revulsion against these men, drawn on a grand scale, who pontificated about art in his grandfather's studio', nevertheless 'the ideas of the Pre-Raphaelites or, perhaps more accurately, their preoccupations stayed with him' (17).[14] His own early experimentations with different types of poetic language and technique reveal a considerable debt to Pre-Raphaelitism and particularly to Rossetti. In his first two volumes, *The Questions at the Well* (1893) and *Poems for Pictures* (1900), Rossettian echoes proliferate, most notably in the love lyrics.[15] In 'October Burden', for example, the use of assonance and compound words recalls Rossetti's style in the sonnets of *The House of Life*:

> Swoon in silent ecstasy.
> Love-lulled let us cling together,
>
> ...
>
> Lean your head upon my breast,
> Love-linked in my arms lie pressed,
> Since in silence Love speaks best.[16]

'Song Dialogue' is clearly derived from Rossetti's 'Even So', using the same song-like question and answer form, although Rossetti is more elliptical and refers more portentously to death and the loss of love:

> So it is, my dear.
> All such things touch secret strings
> For heavy hearts to hear.
> So it is, my dear.

Ford's version reads as follows:

> 'Is it so, my dear?'
> *'Even so!'*
> 'Too much woe to bear?'
> 'Too much woe!'

The title poem of *The Questions at the Well* resembles Morris's writing in *The Defence of Guenevere*, the first and most consistently 'Pre-Raphaelite' collection of his poetry (as well as the one employed by Pater to define 'Aesthetic Poetry').[17] In 'The Questions at the Well', Ford's two medieval lovers linger by moonlight to make their farewells (the man is to leave, presumably to fight in the Hundred Years' War). He confides a disturbing dream to his lover, a vision of 'a deep, drear pit', dropping away to Eternity.[18] At its brink a grinning fiend requires him to answer whether he would cast into the pit either the 'maid thou lovest best' or 'the great broad earth' He is unable to reply but his lover produces the solution: they would not harm the earth's 'Joyous summer mirth' but will eagerly embark on an eternity spent in each other's embrace:

> '... plac[e] thy arms around my neck
> And mine round thee.'

> 'So should we never severed be,
> But kiss and kiss in ecstasy,
> And fall and fall unceasingly,
> Clinging close in dreamy sleep.
> The pit is fathomless and deep
> To all Eternity.'

Love here is medieval in its setting, romantically *contra mundum*, fenced in by fears of death and eternity. In its absolutism it is far from Ford's later idea of 'our terrific, untidy, indifferent empirical age' (*LF* 55). It is also, of course, precisely the aspect of Rossetti's *Paolo and Francesca* which Ford later rejects.

In *Poems for Pictures* Ford turns to the Pre-Raphaelite practice of pictures spawning poems, poems becoming pictures.[19] 'King Cophetua's Wooing', for example, should be read in the light of its painterly inspiration (Burne-Jones's *King Cophetua and the Beggar Maid* of 1884). In 'King Cophetua's Wooing', Ford's drama rests upon a characteristically Pre-Raphaelite 'moment': the decision on the part of the disguised Cophetua to persuade the beggar-maid Christine to be his bride; Christine's discovery of her lover's identity and her acceptance of his astonishing proposal. However, as Stang and Smith observe, Ford makes this Pre-Raphaelite material his own: the two characters 'examine their separate dilemmas in searching for answers to the Fordian question of how best to live: what to give up, what to keep, what price to pay' (130).[20] For Cophetua the moment is hedged about with dreams ('a cloud doth dim my mind'), which Christine attempts to dispel by observing the vibrant reality which surrounds them:

> The larks thrill all above the downs
> With songs
> To shatter dreams.

The antiphonal effect between the lovers differs significantly from that of Rossetti's 'Blessed Damozel', where the lover is exiled in his sorrow and the responses of the 'damozel' fade into ambiguity and can, indeed, be interpreted as imaginary. Ford's Cophetua must engage with another's viewpoint, but he must also return from his idyll to an active world of moral responsibility. Ford's conclusion is sombre and elegiac rather than triumphant, with Christine's reiterated farewells to her past life. The expression of nostalgic regret in her thoughts resembles, perhaps, the introspection of Burne-Jones's painting – as though Ford has interpreted the melancholy of Burne-Jones's figure and created the drama that precedes the frozen moment of the painting.

Ford provides a fascinating insight into the musical and painterly influences on his processes of poetic composition in 'The Making of Modern Verse' (1902).[21] A resonant remembered line, 'She makes me think of lavender', hovers in Ford's mind as he is sitting at the piano, musing over Purcell's elegiac harmonies. The words come back into his mind, 'mixed themselves up with the chromatic sixths and struck a definite "note" – the note of Sir Peter Lely's beauties of Charles II's court, with their long necks, sloping shoulders, painted spinets, virginals, *viols da gamba* or *d'amore*, and the other instruments of an indefinite vanished time'. As the poem develops, Ford alters words for the sake of 'phonetic syzygy', paralleling the repetitions and harmonic variations conventional to a musical lyric:

> *Lavender.*
> You make me think of lavender,
> And that is why I love you so;
> Your sloping shoulders, heavy hair,

And long swan's neck like snow,
Befit those gracious girls of long ago

In defining this evolving of a 'genuine lyric, the "verse for notes of music"', Ford turns to Christina Rossetti. She represents for him 'the high-water mark of pure art', and, through her example, he arrives at a definition of poetry 'as the expression of a mood, in rhythmical language so chosen that no word of the whole can be changed without damage to form and feeling'.[22] D. G. Rossetti's poetry had altered 'the aspect of the modern literary field' and 'enlarged its bounds', but Ford rejected the 'too great profusion ... too much of sweetness, too many jewels' of what he called Rossetti's 'great luxuriance' (*Rossetti* 166). Ford preferred Christina's understated anguish and precision of style. It is this fastidious delineation of conflicting or thwarted desires that led Ford to define her art, in contrast to her brother's, as 'modern'.[23]

III. Pre-Raphaelite Passion

In 1902 Ford selected Rossetti's triptych drawing *Paolo and Francesca*, a 'picture of immense vibrating passion', as an incomparable depiction of love. He is unmoved by the panel depicting punishment ('perhaps because one does not feel convinced of the original sin'), but of the drawing which depicts the fateful kiss he writes:

> ... the definite moment has come and is passing. It is perhaps because that definite moment is so essential, so great, and so necessary a moment in the lives of all men that the picture moves into a plane where technical details, medieval atmospheres, clothes and what one will matter very little ... there is no getting away from the love, the surrender, the moment at the top of a wave of the emotions. (*Rossetti* 64, 66)

Ford was astute in identifying the central and characteristic attitude of Rossetti's paintings as 'a kind of momentary suspense in the midst of intense emotion' (*Rossetti* 60). Rossetti's poetic and visual art both attempt to find ways of arresting the moment, and in Rossetti's work this is always a 'monumental' moment. Although Ford was appreciative of the drawing, his own interest lies elsewhere. As Alan Judd has observed, in seeking 'to render through his writing what he thought important in life', Ford preferred to describe 'the before and after, the effects or mental fall-out of events not directly depicted' (Judd, 32).

In 1911 Ford dedicates an entire chapter of *Ancient Lights* to the topic of 'Pre-Raphaelite Love'. Now, however, he regards 'Pre-Raphaelite Love' as 'a great but rather sloppy emotion'. Again he singles out *Paolo and Francesca* for comment, but his revaluation of 'Pre-Raphaelite Love' produces a quite different reading of the triptych:

> Love, according to the Pre-Raphaelite canon ... was a thing that you swooned about on broad general lines, your eyes closed, your arms outstretched ... and if you weren't sent to hell over it you still drifted about among snow-flakes of fire with your eyes closed and in the arms of the object of your passion. For it is impossible to suppose that when Rossetti painted his picture of Paolo and Francesca in hell, he or any of his admirers thought that these two lovers were really suffering. They were not. They were suffering perhaps with the malaise of love, which is always an uneasiness, but an uneasiness how sweet! ... the lovers were protected by a generalized swooning passion that formed, as it were, a moral and very efficient mackintosh all over them. (*AL* 426)

Ford's rejection here of a 'protective glamour' whereby Pre-Raphaelite adultery escapes the intractable reality of the second circle of hell becomes a thematic and structural element in *Some Do Not . . .*.

In the train journey that commences the tetralogy, Macmaster is working on the proofs of his monograph on Rossetti, and this prompts Tietjens's analogy between English hypocrisy and Pre-Raphaelite Love:

> 'We're always, as it were, committing adultery – like your fellow! – with the name of Heaven on our lips.' (*SDN* 29)

In *Some Do Not . . .*, references to Pre-Raphaelitism – and to Rossetti, in particular – are used to establish the nature of the love affair between Macmaster and Edith Ethel Duchemin and to contrast it with that of Tietjens and Valentine Wannop. Ford, however, is clearly not making a simple contrast between chastity and adultery. He suggests, rather, that the relationship between Tietjens and Valentine – above all, one of integrity – is emblematic of the essential untidiness of modernity. In the penultimate chapter, Tietjens makes an unromantic appeal, 'gasping too, like a fish: "Will you be my mistress tonight?"' (*SDN* 342), and Valentine responds with practical arrangements. This is a rejection of the Rossettian 'moment': it makes what could be romantically absolutist – Ford's subject is, after all, illicit passion in the face of death – clumsy and almost incidental to the muddled business of the day. The affection which slowly develops between Tietjens and Valentine is counter-pointed by the hypocrisy of the adulterous (but 'circumspect') relationship of Macmaster and Edith Ethel. At the same time, there is a degree of the intellectually fastidious in their relationship which also contrasts with the perversity of the Duchemin marriage and the decadent passion of Sylvia Tietjens.

Ford provides a series of clues to associate Rossetti with Duchemin and with Macmaster. Their meeting at the Duchemin breakfast is laden with Pre-Raphaelite references. Macmaster is visiting Duchemin in order to view his Pre-Raphaelite paintings; the canvases displayed being works by Simeon Solomon – 'aureoled, palish heads of ladies carrying lilies that were not very like lilies' (*SDN* 69). For Macmaster, Edith Ethel appears as an incarnation of Pre-Raphaelite womanhood, and he confirms this by quoting 'I looked and saw your eyes in the shadow of your hair' (*SDN* 70). This sounds as if it ought to be a line of verse by Rossetti, but Ford has invented it himself, exaggerating what he dislikes in Rossetti. Duchemin's obscenities at the breakfast table are arrested briefly by Macmaster's request for information about the model for Rossetti's water-colour *Alla Finestra del Cielo*. This is, presumably, a reference to Rossetti's oil-painting *La Donna della Finestra* (1879). Duchemin has witnessed the execution of this painting and supplies the information Macmaster requests: 'Maggie Simpson ... A beautiful girl! ... Very long-necked ... She wasn't of course ... eh ... respectable' (*SDN* 124). However, as with the line of verse and the title (and medium) of the painting, the details here are slightly askew. Jane Morris was the model for Rossetti's painting, but the details Duchemin supplies – the model is now an old woman who has kept a number of pictures – fit better with Fanny Cornforth. There is a destabilising of facticity to mark the fictional world of the novel.

After the humiliation of Duchemin's thundered reference to his 'nuptials', Edith Ethel's tearful confidences to Macmaster produce a climactically sentimental moment, an embrace which Ford frames as in a picture:

> Their lips met in a passion of pity and tears ... He began to see himself: in the tall room, with the long curtains, a round, eagle mirror reflected them gleaming: like a bejewelled picture with great depths; the entwined figures. (*SDN* 129)

Ford transfers to Macmaster's consciousness a compositional device he analyses in Rossetti's painting: the 'device of narrating in a mirror the happenings in the part of the room occupied by the spectator'.[24] He also adopts a Rossettian style for this decisive moment so that the association of their adulterous passion with Pre-Raphaelite love is firmly fixed.

Macmaster's monograph on 'the poet-painter' elicits Tietjens's contempt for what he calls Rossetti's 'polysyllabic Justification by Love' and 'lachrymose polygamy'. (*SDN* 26). In Ford's own monograph on Rossetti, Rossetti is recalled as the magnetic personality whose 'boundless' idealising inspired passionate loyalty. Tietjens is contemptuous of the Rossetti legend:

> ... it revolts me to think of that obese, oily man who never took a bath, in a grease-spotted dressing-gown and the underclothes he's slept in, standing beside a five shilling model with crimped hair, or some Mrs. W. Three Stars, gazing into a mirror that reflects their fetid selves and gilt sunfish and drop chandeliers and plates sickening with cold bacon fat and gurgling about passion. (*SDN* 25)

In this burlesque portrait, Tietjens draws on the same mirror-device, but any possibility of idealisation is blocked by the sordid materiality of the

71

'obese, oily' and unwashed painter, the 'grease-spotted dressing-gown', and the 'cold bacon fat'.[25]

At the end of *Some Do Not* . . ., a half-remembered quotation 'by that detestable fellow' echoes in Tietjens's mind: 'on these debatable borders of the world' (*SDN* 344).[26] At this moment, Macmaster is celebrating his triumph among 'the pictures by that beastly fellow', a blaze of 'bosoms and nipples and lips and pomegranates' (*SDN* 347). Tietjens wants to reject both Rossetti's evocation of liminal worlds and his sensuality, and his objection to the subject of Macmaster's enthusiasm clarifies precisely why 'We're the sort that ... *do not*!' (*SDN* 346). The voluptuous decadence of Rossetti's late paintings gives way to memories of the figure of a 'decent' Tommie who 'didn't get his girl into trouble before going to be killed' (*SDN* 334).

IV. The Femme Fatale

In re-defining his attitude towards Pre-Raphaelite passion, Ford was also moving away from a symbolic art towards an engagement with the apparent shapelessness of life. One aspect of this change was the eschewing of the 'moment' and the foregrounding of 'the before and after'. It might almost be said that, for Ford in his later work, the 'moment' must *not* be pregnant with meaning. By comparison, his first novel, *The Shifting of the Fire* (1892), constructs its melodramatic plot around three 'moments' of epiphanic significance, each marked by the motif indicated in the title.[27] At the beginning of the novel, Edith Rylands is awaiting her fiancé in 'an ecstasy of expectation' (*SF* 3-4). As he enters the house, a violent storm outside is swept into the room with 'a great burst of sound'. Hollebone passes from the 'tumult' outside to the dark room where Edith waits in silence. He is unconscious, at first, of her presence:

> ... for some moments silence reigned supreme; but suddenly the fire shifted – a blaze of flame shot upwards. By its light the girl became plainly visible. (*SF* 4)

On the second occasion, the wind is again 'shrieking shrilly', 'wailing and throbbing mournfully, like a soul longing after the impossible' (*SF* 236). This is clearly a warning to Hollebone. By this point, he has learned of Edith's marriage; he has resolved that he should loathe her; and he is about to declare his love for his cousin Kate. At this moment, the fire shifts, and, as it shifts, 'a flickering flame danced and trembled and then died away, and with it died away his love for the silent figure that it lit up for the moment' (*SF* 237). Ford's final use of the motif occurs as Edith's husband, Kasker-Ryves, waits for death. He too sits in darkness in the anticipation that the dying embers of the fire will yield one final vision of the face that he has loved. Smith and Stang have described this novel as 'saturated' in Wagner and Berlioz (134), and the title of the novel can certainly be interpreted as a musical *idée fixe*. However, Ford also introduces a cluster of Rossettian allusions: Edith is described as 'rather like one of Rossetti's pictures'; Hollebone and Lord Tatton discuss *The Blessed Damozel*; Hollebone's poem to Edith refers to Rossetti's sonnet 'Body's Beauty'. Paul Wiley has suggested that *The Shifting of the Fire* is an attempt to 'rid passion' of 'pre-Raphaelite sanctions' (Wiley, 135). Hollebone's poem, however, draws on Rossetti to predict the anguish that love will bring him. Compare his lines ('My love did send to me a single strand/ From her great golden Heav'n of hair/ ... Alas! the treacherous hair twines round my heart' [*SF* 225]) with Rossetti's 'Body's Beauty', where Lilith destroys her lover by twining 'round his heart one strangling golden hair'.[28]

The 'Half Moon' (written in 1907) and *The Young Lovell* (1913) can also justifiably be seen as late Pre-Raphaelite works through their use of the figure of the 'belle dame sans merci'. *The 'Half Moon'* is informed by Anne Jeal's demonology. She is a characteristically Pre-Raphaelite sorceress in her single-minded desire to destroy the man she loves. Ford begins the novel with a tableau which functions as a proleptic pictorial prologue to the action: Anne Jeal attempts to 'charm' Edward Colman, as she wills him to glance in her direction; when she does not succeed and he looks towards the home of her rival, Magdalena, Anne improvises a gallows for two mannikin figures and commits herself to accomplishing both of their deaths.[29]

In his study of Rossetti, Ford singled out for attention *The Laboratory* (1849), a small water-colour dating from the early Pre-Raphaelite period.[30] The painting illustrates Browning's poem by depicting an elaborately-dressed court lady procuring an alchemist's poison to murder a rival. Ford comments that this 'moment of intense passion' typifies Rossetti's 'essentially dramatic spirit', and he admires the 'whole atmosphere' of Rossetti's picture – 'one of illicit passion in a closed space' (*Rossetti* 38). This is an effect which Ford evokes at the beginning of *The 'Half Moon'* and in the many dark, secluded scenes which follow. Ford further achieves an effect characteristic of Rossetti in exploiting the contrast between the fair, devout submissive Magdalena and Anne's bold and animated sexuality. However, it is Anne's witchcraft which occasions one of the most dramatic set pieces of the novel and reveals how far Ford's narrative technique in *The 'Half Moon'* draws on the art of painting. Ford creates a highly melodramatic scene: Anne bares her breast; invokes Belcabrae, the wife of Satan; incants blasphemous prayers; and, finally, stabs herself – smiling – in the breast. But this drama is interrupted by the inconsequential information that, as she speaks, 'her voice wandered away among the dark pillars of the bed, the dark hangings, the dark presses that had carved on them the arms of the Queen Anne Boleyn, painted in red and gold and blue, but very much faded' (*HM* 176). Ford is here offering a narrative translation of Rossetti's method in his medieval water-colours. Ford's analysis of this method draws attention to the 'astonishingly real' pictorial detail which combines with 'half wilful exaggeration' (*Rossetti* 94) to produce an art which 'appeals very intimately ... if we will enter the door which it holds open for us' (*Rossetti* 96).

Ford's interest, in *The 'Half Moon'*, lies in the conflict and torment Anne experiences in systematically destroying the man she loves. In *The Young Lovell*, Ford once more uses the Pre-Raphaelite *femme fatale* in an historical fantasy. The novel is set in Northumberland in 1486, but Lovell's vigil, with which it begins, evokes a mysterious supernatural world which appears to fuse Flaubert's *La tentation de Saint Antoine* with a more homely folk tradition of crepuscular mysteries. Ford claimed to have conceived *The Young Lovell* as a 'pretty big and serious historical work' (*LF* 56), but it is really a fantasy dealing with the faery enchantment of the young knight. His focus is not so much the *femme fatale* as the destructive effects of passion. Because of 'the lady of the doves and sparrows' (*YL* 219), the world to which Lovell returns seems unreal to him, and his fiancée, Margaret, has become 'wearisome beyond endurance'. As Saunders observes, 'the power of sexuality de-realizes and disturbs all commitments and stabilities' (I, 384).

The culmination of Ford's interest in the destructive female is Sylvia Tietjens, who can be seen to embody Rossetti's archetypal *femme fatale*. Rossetti made Lilith the subject of both painting and poetry. Ford described her as 'the witch-wife of Adam', who 'stood for illicit love, for the women who bring sorrow to the Eves of this world and disaster to the hearth' (*Rossetti* 140). In *The House of Life*, Rossetti offered the following account of her destructive desires:

> Of Adam's first wife, Lilith, it is told
> [That] her enchanted hair was the first gold.
> And still she sits, young while the earth is old,
>   And, subtly of herself contemplative,
>   Draws men to watch the bright web she can weave,
> Till heart and body and life are in its hold.[31]

Aesthetic and decadent images accrue around Sylvia Tietjens. She is connected with Wagner's Venusberg music and with Burne-Jones 'La Belle Dame Sans Merci'.[32] But Tietjens sees her in terms which clearly recall Rossetti's Lilith:

> ... coiled up on a convent bed. ... Hating. ... Her certainly glorious hair all round her. ... Hating. ... (*NMP* 82)

If Ford is rejecting what was widely perceived to be Pre-Raphaelite decadence through his depiction of Sylvia Tietjens, he is also reinventing Rossetti for the Tietjens novels. Ford thus makes a complex rapprochement with his Pre-Raphaelite childhood, a rapprochement that combines an openly antagonistic engagement with a deeply-informed exploitation of his inheritance.

NOTES

1.'The Millais and Rossetti Exhibitions', *Fortnightly Review*, 69 (Feb. 1898), 196.

2. *Contemporary Review*, 74 (Aug. 1898), 193.

3. Ann Barr Snitow, *Ford Madox Ford and the Voice of Uncertainty*, Baton Rouge: University of Louisiana State University Press, 1984, p. 8.

4. Kestner suggests that this work should be read as a protonovel, a 'proleptic text in which one can see the formation of the Fordian alienated protagonist'. See Joseph A. Kestner, 'Ford Madox Ford as a Critic of the Pre-Raphaelites',*Contemporary Literature*, 30:2 (Summer 1989), 224-37.

5. Franz Hueffer wrote an introductory Memoir for the Tauchnitz edition of Rossetti's poems (1873).

6. Fredeman judges Ford's work to be 'perhaps the best of the early studies of the movement ... [In] attempting to clarify some of the debatable points concerning the history of the Brotherhood, he does succeed in catching the spirit which animated the original group'. See W. E. Fredeman, *Pre-Raphaelitism: A Bibliocritical Study*, Harvard University Press, 1965, p. 26.

7. As Saunders points out, he also here first articulates a distinction between the Pre-Raphaelites, who 'gave to material phases of Nature a relative permanence', and Impressionists, who sought 'that delicious sense of swift change, that poetry of varying moods, of varying lights, of varying shadows' (I, 232).

8. The first volume of the *English Review*, however, included accounts of Rossetti and Morris at Kelmscott by Watts-Dunton and at Cheyne Walk by Meredith; a caricature drawing of Rossetti by Ford Madox Brown; and the first publication of Rossetti's macabre ballad 'Jan Van Hunks'.

9. Wiley, p. 27; Kestner, p. 224.

10. *The Bookman*, 40 (June 1911), 113-120, 118.

11. Ford makes clear elsewhere what he meant by 'Prussianised': 'I hate Prussia for her efficiency, for her commercial spirit, for her commercial dishonesty ... Prussia [does] not contain the birthplace of a single poet, humanist, artist, or decent human being' (*The Outlook* [29 August 1914], 270, 271).

12. Kenneth Rexroth, Introduction,*Buckshee*, xvii. Stella Bowen similarly observes that Ford was 'full of stories ... Swinburne, Rossetti ...' (*Drawn from Life*, London: Collins, 1941, p. 62).

13. Max Saunders, 'A Life in Writing: Ford Madox Ford's Dispersed Autobiographies', *Antaeus*, 56 (Spring 1986), 47-69, 60.

14. Saunders more accurately describes the emotion Ford experienced as 'fear' rather than revulsion (I, 31).

15. These similarities include the use of chivalric vocabulary, the creation of a mood of nostalgic reverie, and various verbal echoes.

16. See Dante Gabriel Rossetti, *The Works*, London: Ellis, 1911.

17. Pater's essay was first published in the *Westminster Review* (October 1868) and re-printed in *Appreciations*, London: Macmillan, 1889.

18. A memory, perhaps, of 'the Pit of Fortune's Wheel' in Rossetti's 'The King's Tragedy'.

19. Pater had drawn on Rossetti's 'Sonnets on Pictures' to examine such inter-relationships. See 'The School of Giorgione' in D. L. Hill (ed.), *The Renaissance: Studies in Art and Poetry*, London: University of California Press, 1980, p. 105.

20. Sondra J. Stang and Carl Smith, '"Music for a While": Ford's Compositions for Voice and Piano', *Contemporary Literature*, 30:2 (Summer 1989); an abridged version appeared as 'Ford's Musical Compositions' in *Agenda*, 27:4-28:1 (Winter 1989/Spring 1990), 120-38, 130.

21. 'The Making of Modern Verse', *The Academy and Literature*, 62: I, 19 April 1902, 412-14; II, 26 April 1902, 438-9.

22. I, p. 413. Robert Lowell asserts that Ford's own poetry never attained this ideal, because Ford was 'Pre-Raphaelite to the heart': 'the soul of the old dead style remains to

hamper him' (*Buckshee*). Nevertheless, Ford's evolving definition of poetry leads directly, as Hampson has shown, into Pound's 'imagist' programme. Consider the imagist requirement: 'To use absolutely no word that does not contribute to the presentation' (quoted, Hampson, p. 102).

23. See Paul Skinner's essay below.

24. Ford observes that this was 'a trick much beloved by both Rossetti and Madox Brown' and notes its 'singularly effective' use in Rossetti's *Lucrezia* (*Rossetti* 107).

25. Ford is here recycling the story of Henry James's visit to Rossetti's studio. According to Ford, James mistook the garment in which Rossetti painted for a dressing-gown, and deduced from it that Rossetti was 'disgusting in his habits, never took baths, and was insupportably lecherous' (*RY* 15). 'Greasy ham' also features in this account.

26. The quotation is taken from 'Youth's Spring Tribute', *The House of Life* XIV. Ford had praised this sonnet for describing 'things really and brilliantly *seen*' rather than just presenting 'a catalogue of pictures of Abstract Ideas' (*Rossetti* 168).

27. Moser reads this motif as a symbol of passion, which impels people as it consumes them. See Thomas Moser, *The Life in the Fiction of Ford Madox Ford*, Princeton: Princeton University Press, 1980.

28. *The House of Life*, LXXVIII.

29. Compare Rossetti's 'Sister Helen', where Helen is occupied in melting a wax image of her lover; the spell has taken three days to mature and is nearing completion at the start of the poem.

30. See Virginia Surtees, *The Paintings and Drawings of Dante Gabriel Rossetti*, Oxford: Clarendon Press, 1971, Text 41, Plate 25.

31. 'Body's Beauty', *The House of Life*, LXXVIII, 100.

32. Perowne compares Sylvia to 'a picture that my mother's got, by Burne-Jones ... A cruel looking woman with a distant smile ... Some vampire ... La belle Dame sans Merci ...' (*NMP* 151). Keats's poems were a favourite source for Pre-Raphaelite art, but Burne-Jones did not execute a picture on this theme. Rossetti did. Burne-Jones painted other *femmes fatales*.

POOR DAN ROBIN:

FORD MADOX FORD'S POETRY

Paul Skinner

When other Bards sing mortal loud, like swearing,
Like poor Dan Robin, thankful for your crumb
If the wind lulls I try to get a hearing (*LF* 99)[1]

Readers of Ford Madox Ford's work – not to mention that of his
contemporaries and critics – are accustomed to being confronted by a
bewildering variety of Fords. Apart from the novelist, the critic, the
editor and the autobiographer, the most familiar include the 'godfather'
of '*les jeunes*', the preacher of 'prose' and the instigator – most famously
of Ezra Pound. And Ford the poet? Very little recent criticism has
concerned itself with that aspect of his writings. Is this because his
poetry is of little value, or not to contemporary taste, or because the
poetry itself has been obscured by Ford's role in the poetic careers of
others? In this essay I want to review that role, to reconsider Ford's work
in the context of Imagism, Futurism and Vorticism, and to examine, or
re-examine, his criteria of 'modern poetry'.

Ford was a copious writer. His 1936 *Collected Poems* excludes the
book-length *Mister Bosphorus and the Muses* yet runs to 348 pages, and
my discussion of the poetry is inevitably highly selective. I may also
note here that, while there is no poetic masterpiece equivalent to *The
Good Soldier* or *Parade's End* or *It Was the Nightingale*, I believe that
almost every volume of poetry by Ford contains poems of value. The
question remains, I suppose, the criteria by which that value is
estimated: and such criteria are, in part, those which Ford helped to
establish and, in part – 'compression', 'hardness', 'intensity' – those he
did not.

I. The Good Soldier Among the Isms

Writing to Ford Madox Ford from St Raphael in January 1921, Ezra Pound enclosed a letter from F. S. Flint, in which Flint invited Pound to contribute a rough draft of 'our joint screed' on Imagism. 'Am now sending him an outline for a book – or very nearly a book', Pound commented;[2] but, in his reply to Flint, he had also proposed that Flint write a critique of Ford, 'whose impressionism probably agrees with your own attitude'. And this attitude was, Pound added, in opposition to his own emphasis on vortex, concentration, condensation, hardness.[3]

Six months earlier, Ford had written to Pound: 'I think it important that we should agree on a formula for vers libre, non-representationalism and other things before I go any further. We want some manifestoes ...' He added: 'You forget that it is six years since I poured oil on these eaux puantes and I don't so hell of a well rem[e]mber who were Imagistes and what it was all about' (*LF* 118). Pound responded with an epistolary lecture on 'vers libre etc.',[4] and Ford subsequently devoted an article, later a chapter of *Thus to Revisit*, to 'Mr. Pound, Mr. Flint, Some Imagistes or Cubists, and the Poetic Vernacular'.

Ford's 'six years' returns us to 1914, when publication of *Des Imagistes* and *Blast* prompted his assiduous attention to 'les jeunes' in the columns of *The Outlook*: in July of the following year, Pound wrote to Flint to point out 'errors' of fact in Flint's 'History of Imagism' ('BULLSHIT') under five headings, the first 'correction' being that 'the drive towards simple current speech' had come from Ford. In his reply, Flint commented that:

> The whole drive towards simple current speech does not come from F.M.H. He was one of the generals of division in an army composed of many divisions. No doubt his operations seem of paramount importance to you because you were enrolled under him. All the same, it was an omission on my part not to have mentioned his influence on you: it shall be repaired.[5]

Flint's phrasing is careful: his denial that the *whole* of the drive towards 'simple current speech' derives from Ford responds to a claim that Pound did not explicitly make, while 'his influence on you' begs the question of Ford's place in the history of Imagism because Pound's centrality to that history is precisely the issue. ('Divisions' is also good, and 'enrolled' a pleasing though – presumably – unintended pun for historians of the Giessen Roll).[6] Flint's partisan support for the 'forgotten school of 1909' impelled him towards unrealistic claims on their behalf, but his bitterness about what he saw as Pound's diminution of Flint's own role in mapping the 'approach to Paris' was not wholly unjustified.[7] To those not travelling at a comparable rate of speed in this period, Pound often appeared to *snatch*.

In fact, Flint's 'History' is not at all concerned with 'simple current speech'. It mentions *vers libre*, 'the Image', *tanka* and *haikai*, and cites T. E. Hulme's insistence on 'absolutely accurate presentation and no verbiage', but mentions neither language nor content. And while Edward Storer, Hulme and Flint himself had indeed written poems in colloquial language, Pound was surely correct in ascribing to Ford the main credit for that 'drive'. As early as 1900 or 1901, Ford had stressed his dislike of a 'professional-poetic dialect', and commented on Wordsworth's choice 'not so much of words as of language', and his bothering too little with 'the search for the just word,'[8] while he had been urging the drawing of 'concrete pictures, leaving your hearer to draw the morals', since at least 1904.[9] In a 1907 article, he had remarked that '[i]n Germany, even more than in England, there is a written language and a spoken. The spoken language is direct, forcible and simple; the written is involved, pompous, and full of archaisms,'[10] while, in January 1908, he recalled his old schoolmaster's maxim: 'Schreib wie du sprichst!', which he termed 'a glorious but impracticable doctrine' while identifying it, nevertheless, as 'the moral that I wish to append to this series of articles.'[11]

This is not a matter of a few stray remarks but, rather, a sustained programme – *videlicet*, a 'drive'. Ford's most famous formulation of his poetics is, of course, the 'Preface' to his 1913 *Collected Poems*. In September 1912, Ezra Pound wrote to his fiancée, Dorothy Shakespear, commenting on the helpfulness of Ford's criticisms and remarking: 'I doubt not that life is as the sages have agreed "Just one damn thing after another" and our only recourse is to watch the procession as stoically as possible'.[12] Those 'sages' can, perhaps, be whittled down to 'an American cartoon' which Ford recalled seeing, representing 'a dog pursuing a cat out of the door of a particularly hideous tenement house, and beneath this picture was inscribed the caption: "This is life – one damn thing after another"' (*CP1* 31, 20). That word 'procession' is also suggestive: in his preface, Ford quoted Heine's 'Wahlfart nach Kevelaar':

> Denn nach Köln am Rheine
> Geht die Procession

to advance the ironic claim that it was impossible to 'use the word procession in an English poem. It would not be literary' (*CP1* 12); this, of course, before using it in the opening poem of the book.[13] Ford's point was that a moribund and absurdly limited poetic language had handed over great areas of 'ordinary experience' to the realistic novelists, and that the recovery by the poets of contemporary life was best begun by a renovation of poetic diction, or rather, elimination of it altogether. 'The actual language – the vernacular employed – is a secondary matter,' Ford wrote: but he knew the two were inextricable. 'I prefer personally the language of my own day, a language clear enough for certain matters, employing slang where slang is felicitous and vulgarity where it seems to me that vulgarity is the only weapon against dullness' (*CP1* 12).

Clearly, Ford's 'drive' is towards something more than a reform of diction, more even than the elimination of the 'moralizing' tendency. Not only language and tone are involved here but subject too. George Moffat, the protagonist of Ford's 1905 novel, *The Benefactor*, remarks of poetry that it needs 'commonplaces' (*B* 104), and, in his 1907 article on Maurice Hewlett, Ford expressed the desire that Hewlett be 'his real self' and present his image of 'the possibilities of [modern] life; we do not nearly so much want to know what life might have been like had there been giants in the old days.'[14] In December of that year, Ford's

description of a scene he had witnessed outside the Tottenham Court
Road Tube Station (clearly foreshadowing Pound's later account of the
genesis of 'In a Station of the Metro') concluded:

> And the cold, the suggestion of terror, of light, and of life ... It was not
> Romance – it was Poetry. It was the Poetry of the normal, of the usual, the
> poetry of the innumerable little efforts of mankind ... But of that I find little
> in the work of living novelists, and less or nothing in the work of living
> poets.[15]

In his 'quarrel with modern verse', Ford criticized much of it for
dealing 'in a derivative manner with mediaeval emotions', asserting that:
'We live in our day, we live in our time, and he is not a proper man who
will not look in the face his day and his time' (*CA* 187). He prophesied
the time when 'some young poets get it into their heads to come out of
their book-closets and take ... a walk down Fleet Street, or a ride on the
top of a 'bus from Shepherd's Bush to Poplar' (*CA* 190), and, in the same
month, his review of Flint's *In the Net of the Stars* observed that:

> Mr Flint occasionally attempts to render some of the aspects of modern life.
> And it is from such rendering that – if ever it will – poetry will once more
> regain its hold upon the attentions of the English-speaking world. We wish
> Mr Flint would accept the conditions in which he lives with more composure
> and see in them the poetry that exists now as in every other age. But it is
> better to look at modern life and to hate it than never to have looked at it at
> all.[16]

Of Christina Rossetti, Ford remarked that, 'within the bounds of her
personal emotions ... she expressed herself consummately' and 'in this ...
proved herself a poet more modern than her brother ...' (*MI* 60-1). Ford
noted that Christina's nature was 'mediaeval in the sense that it cared for
little things and for arbitrary arrangements. In the same sense it was so
very modern. For the life of to-day is more and more becoming a life of
little things' (*MI* 68-9). He went on to note 'an end of generalisations, the
loss of the sense of a whole, the feeling of a grand design'. Christina

Rossetti's poetry might be almost altogether introspective, but then, Ford concluded, 'all modern poetry must be almost altogether introspective' (*MI* 65).

Ford's own artistic lineage led to (among other things) a strong distrust of the poet as great figure and an emphasis instead upon 'a man speaking to men'.[17] His 1914 review of Yeats remembers his youthful view of that poet and the irritation caused by Yeats's 'Lake Isle of Innisfree'. Being, 'presumably even at that early age, a prose impressionist', Ford noted, he would have preferred the poem to run:

At Innesfree [sic] there is a public-house;
They board you well for ten and six a week.

The mutton is not good, but you can eat
Their honey. I am going there to take
A week or so of holiday to-morrow.

'There might have been in addition some details about the landscape and whether the fishing was good,' Ford added. 'That was what I wanted in a poem of those days; that is what I still want in a poem.'[18]

Commonplaces; the poetry of the ordinary; little things; concrete pictures; colloquial language. But there is another, more specific, criterion of 'the modern' that Ford alludes to more than once. In 'Pure Literature', written in the second half of 1922, he refers to Robert Herrick, 'who wrote in effect: "Give me my city life that I may live" and was to that extent modern'.[19] And, reviewing *Des Imagistes*, Ford had drawn attention to 'the very beautiful poems of Mr. Flint, which are upon the whole most what I want, since they are about this city.'[20]

It seems, on the face of it, an odd criterion. Yet by the time *Des Imagistes* appeared, Ford may well have felt that the argument for plain language and *vers libre* was already effectively won.[21] Many of these 'Imagiste' poems, though, were concerned with Greek myth, the gods, 'Sinetic' pictures. Many were also very short, and Ford saw no inherent virtue in compression. His own poems were 'longish things':[22] he needed space, the rhythms of speech, the conversational sentence. His effects were cumulative, his own version of 'intensity' customarily focused on, precisely, an 'effect', one achieved in the reader's mind. When he noted that 'Liu Ch'e' was 'a tiny novel', he perceived an evocative situation, the elements of an 'affair', as Pound did in 'The Jewel Stairs' Grievance', which moved him to write an excited footnote, numbering almost twice as many words as the poem itself contained. But what could one make of this:

> The petals fall in the fountain,
> the orange-coloured rose-leaves,
> Their ochre clings to the stone. ('Ts'ai Chi'h')

Ford was not, that is to say, centrally concerned with 'the Image'. He was interested in 'good writing', in 'prose values', in *vers libre*, in 'London of the nineteen tens', content 'to endure the rattles and the bangs', and hoping to see them 'rendered.'[23] But that 'rendering' must voice 'the life of dust, toil, discouragement, excitement and enervation that I and many millions lead to-day' (*CP1* 28) and, in Ford's view, most of the Imagiste poems failed to do this.

In 1913, Ford alluded to 'the sort of Futurist picture that life is to me and my likes' (*CP1* 27), seeming to regard the Futurists as essentially 'representational', impressionist and 'really realists', doing:

> very much what novelists of the type of Flaubert or short-story writers of the type of Maupassant aimed at. They gave you not so much the reconstitution of a crystallised scene in which all the figures were arrested ... as fragments of impressions gathered during a period of time, during a period of emotion, or during a period of travel.[24]

Such comparisons imply Ford's own alignment with Futurism ('there is not a single word of Mr Marinetti's doctrines that I have not been preaching since I was fifteen ...'). Writing just after the eventual publication of *Blast*, Ford remarked that: 'Signor Marinetti in theory – like myself in practice – is a materialist ... Cubists, Vorticists, and the rest of them are in fact visionaries; Post-Impressionists, Impressionists, Futurists and the rest of us are materialists ...' While, as 'a conférencier', Marinetti was 'unequalled,' he was 'in no sense an artist of a creative kind' and his poems were 'a nuisance'. Ford's ironic praise of the Futurists is selective: the 'doctrine' that Marinetti has 'got hold of' is that 'the important thing to think about is our own time and our own clime ... Our own day is more of a Golden Age than any other age ever was ...'[25]

Ford confessed to inclining towards the Futurists 'just because they want to smash things', observing that 'what we want most of all in the literature of to-day is religion, is intolerance, is persecution, and not the mawkish flapdoodle of culture, Fabianism, peace, and good will.'[26] This jeremiad was, in the first instance, political: Ford saw Liberalism and Fabianism as conducing to a new grey world of standardization, statistics and bloodless indifference. But the sentiment, if not the phrasing, was shared by many, of varying political persuasions.

Ford would have been repelled by the 'machinolatry' of the Futurists, and would not subscribe to 'the beauty of speed', the violent exclusion of 'the past' or the fierce nationalism that the Italians adopted. Yet he might well be drawn to the strong visual element in Marinetti's early manifestoes and the insistence upon contemporary urban actualities; and it is noticeable that, when he discusses Futurism, Ford frequently employs such words as 'effect' and 'spectator', that he sees in Futurism the crucial interaction between artist or artwork and audience which he suspected the Vorticists of dismissing.

It is, of course, the sense of that interaction which lies behind or beneath so many of Ford's critical pronouncements, which even seems, to some critics, to render him 'unmodernist'.[27] In the 'Preface', Ford wrote of the German poets:

These fellows you know. They sit at their high windows in German lodgings; they lean out; it is raining steadily. Opposite them is a shop where herring salad, onions and oranges are sold. A woman with a red petticoat and a black and grey check shawl goes into the shop and buys three onions, four oranges and half a kilo of herring salad. And there is a poem! Hang it all! There is a poem. (*CP1* 12)

Though not, we might add, a Ford poem. Here is Ford:

> I went down 'twixt tobacco and grain,
> Descending the chequer board plain
> Where the apples and maize are;
> Under the loopholed gate
> In the village wall
> Where the goats clatter over the cobbles
> And the intricate straw-littered ways are ...
> The ancient watchman hobbles
> Cloaked, with his glasses of horn at the end of his nose,
> Wearing velvet short hose
> And a three-cornered hat on his pate,
> And his pike-staff and all.
> And [...]   ('The Starling': *CP1* 34)

And? '[I]t is absolutely the devil,' as Pound wrote, in a passage often cited, 'to try to quote snippets from a man whose poems are gracious impressions, leisurely, low-toned.'[28] And 'low-toned' is, to be sure, *le mot juste*. 'I suppose,' Ford writes:

> that what I have been aiming at all my life is a literary form that will produce the effect of a quiet voice going on talking and talking, without much ejaculation, without the employment of any verbal strangeness – just quietly saying things.[29]

It is a stratagem familiar to John Dowell: 'And I shall go on talking in a low voice while the sea sounds in the distance and overhead the great black flood of wind polishes the bright stars' (*GS* 17). That is the real right – Fordian – thing. The low voice talking beneath or against those louder noises: whether of clamorous Vorticists, booming Victorian poets or the sea and 'the great black flood of wind.' Indeed, *The Good Soldier* (which is, surely, *inter alia*, an extended parody of a late

87

Jamesian sentence), should be seen in precisely this context. Against the explosive sounds of Vorticism, Ford sets a highly crafted text (though in an 'oral' mode), which is profoundly concerned with speech and silence, and which, while detailing deaths, madness, betrayal and suicide, hardly raises its voice. Eschewing the stasis and 'timeless' qualities of Imagisme, the novel engages with the dynamics of memory and intricate causality. And when Ford, reviewing the contents of *Blast*, remarks that '[o]f work in the past method there is ... a portion of a novel by myself which appears rather unexciting when I see it in print', something more than modesty is involved. The 'excitement' of *The Good Soldier* does not derive from typographical innovation, the *look* of the work on the page; Ford's text compels the reader's total engagement: not merely of sight, but of mind and 'heart' also. *Turdus philomelos* is not *erithacus rubecula*.[30] Nevertheless, while Ford's novel 'was no louder than a thrush in the pages of *Blast*' (*RY* 419), we may surmise that 'poor Dan Robin' did not intend that it should be.

In early 1915, reviewing some of the 'simple and now obvious ideas' of the decade thus far which seemed to him 'to be the motifs of the Renaissance', and the names of 'men who embody them,' Pound ascribed to Ford 'the belief that poetry should be as well written as prose, and that "good prose is just your conversation."'[31] 'Just your conversation': a dangerous statement to be let loose among the uninitiated, with *The Good Soldier* not yet available, *in toto*, to underwrite it. 'Good prose', at any rate – and good poetry? Because surely that sense, not just of 'saying things' but of *conversation*, vitally including the other person, and not just particular or even habitual conversations, between Ford and Conrad, Ford and Pound, but conversation as mode, as measure, is of absolutely central significance to all of Ford's work. He recollected arriving at the 'definite theory' that 'what I was trying to attain to was verse that was like one's intimate conversation with someone one loved very much' (*TR* 213).[32] And one example of that conversation, extending over years, is recalled by Ford thus:

... our collaboration [between Ford and Conrad] was almost purely oral. We wrote and read aloud the one to the other. Possibly in the end we even wrote *to* read aloud the one to the other.   (*NC* 11; see also *JC* 203)

Ford differentiated his own work from that of the other poets represented in *Des Imagistes* in just this way. In 1914 he considered 'the unit of vers libre' to be 'really the conversational sentence of the author' (and, as such, 'the most intimate means of expression').[33] In *Thus to Revisit*, he would describe his own contribution to the *Des Imagistes* anthology as 'more conversational' than other poems he quoted, by Pound, H. D., Flint and Williams: 'it has the sound rather of a man talking amiably to just any company ... the other Imagistes ... seem to be writing very simple and carefully chosen words, sparingly, for incision on alabaster' (*TR* 159). But he also refers to Pound's most famous short poem in this context:

> So the Vorticists and others proceeded on their clamorous ways ... They abolished not only the Illusion of the Subject, but the Subject itself ... They gave you dashes and whirls of pure colour; words washed down till they were just Mr. Pound's
> Petals on a wet black bough (*TR* 140)

'[W]ords washed down' is a curious phrase. Ford suggests that 'what most characterised [the Imagistes'] products was a sort of cleanness ... The work is free of the polysyllabic, honey-dripping and derivative adjectives that ... makes nineteenth-century poetry as a whole seem greasy and "close" ...' (*TR* 157). Yet he implies that the cleaning process has been too severe, its agents a little too abrasive, that, perhaps, something better retained has been thrown out with the water.

The most striking distinction Ford makes is that between 'the sound ... of a man talking ... to just any company' and 'writing ... for incision on alabaster'. Ford's first instance is both oral and aural, connoting both speaker and listener; the second is textual and visual, implying fixity and permanence. But it also carries the inescapable connotation of inscribed laws; and Pound himself observed of his 'LIST OF DON'TS' that he could not 'put all of them into Mosaic negative'.[34]

> The "age demanded" chiefly a mould in plaster,
> Made with no loss of time,
> A prose kinema, not, not assuredly, alabaster
> Or the "sculpture" of rhyme.[35]

So Pound wrote in 1919-1920, looking back to the high period of Imagisme and Vorticism, less in sorrow than in anger. But certainly his early formulations of Imagiste precepts were remarkable for their negative emphases, in this first, essentially critical, phase, a paring away of fat or slack. Of Pound's own poems in *Des Imagistes*, Ford would have known 'Δώρια' and 'The Return' from *Ripostes*; beyond these, four other poems – three of them transformations of versions by H. A. Giles – totalled just twenty-two lines. Unsurprisingly, Ford remarked that 'one end of this volume is Hellenic, the other extremity Sinetic, if that be the proper term for things which show a Chinese influence.' And 'the middle regions' – where, surely, Ford situated himself? They contained 'the very beautiful poems of Mr. Flint'.

II: Talking in a Low Voice

And to what extent does Ford's own poetry reflect his advance towards the position taken up in the 'Preface' and his other critical writings of that period?

When the early poems succeed, they do so for the most part, in musical and rhythmical terms but also, I suspect, for the modern reader, in largely negative ones: as in the case of Pound, we are always half-consciously looking for that moment when the archaisms and inversions and 'poetic' awkwardnesses are notable only for their absence, when they give way to clarity, simplicity and cleanness of phrasing.

> The firelight gilds the patterns on the walls,
> The yellow flames fly upwards from the brands,
> On fold and farm the sad grey twilight falls,

And shrouds the downs and hides the hollow lands.

Well enough, if metrically unexciting, the small alliterative clusters and assonance ('shrouds ... downs') not obtrusive. But the second stanza begins:

And pensive is the hour ('Gray: For a Picture': *CP1* 146)

an inversion it may seem uncharitable to inveigh against but the more easily discernible because the ear and eye are alert to precisely such lapses. 'You see I hate – and I hated then – inversions of phrase. A line like *A sensitive plant in a garden grew* filled me with hot rage' (*CW* 157). So Ford wrote – or said – some time in the post-war decade. But a few years earlier, he observed that he had 'thought about verse desultorily before 1912' and that it was 'not until about 1915 or 1916' that he 'devoted really the whole of [his] aesthetic mind to the practical side of verse-writing' (*TR* 129). And certainly, in many respects and for several years, his poetic practice lagged behind his critical pronouncements, an observation that has also been made, with some justice, about his novels.

Such weaknesses of word order and diction are, however, less obviously present in Ford's 'dialect' poems or those lyrics which are frankly 'songs':

Come up from the field,
Come up from the fold,
For the farmer has broken,
His things must be sold.   ('Auctioneer's Song': *CP1* 153)

And, in most of these 'songs', Ford seems generally more at ease:

Al'ington Knoll's a mound a top,
With a dick all round and it's bound to stop,
For them as made it in them old days
Sees to it well that theer it stays ... ('Aldington Knoll': *CP1* 154)

And beyond the 'songs'? 'On a Marsh Road' is most often noted now because Pound chose its eighth line as a negative example ('dim lands of peace') of mixing 'an abstraction with the concrete';[36] yet we can see what may have drawn his attention to the poem in the first place:

> A bluff of cliff, purple against the south,
> And nigh one shoulder-top an orange pane.
> This wet, clean road; clear twilight held in the pools,
> And ragged thorns, ghost reeds and dim, dead willows. (*CP1* 135)

'Held in pools' would sustain a uniformity of metre at that stage: but the slight irregularity is subtly effective. So too is the disyllabic 'willows' in the last line. Here, as in so much of his writing, Ford foregrounds a conventional or wholly regular form only to depart from that initial model, often obliquely, or with an artful subtlety. He exploits, of course, an analogous strategy, though with a far greater and more varied power, in his novels, where he so often achieves an extraordinary resonance while presenting his materials in a manner perfectly consonant with the tenets of realism.

By 1912, Ford had written 'To All the Dead':

> But I sat there, and a friendly Yankee
> Was lecturing me on the nature of things
> (It's a way Americans have!) He was cranky,
> Just as much as his rooms and his chairs and his tables.
> But the window stood open and over the way
> I saw that the house with the modernest facings
> Had an old tiled roof with mansards and gables.
> It housed a jeweller, two modistes,
> A vendor of fans; and the topmost sign
> Announced in a golden double line
> A salon of Chinese chiropodists. (*CP1* 40)

Some of the rhythms tend to canter; the exigencies of rhyme – 'cranky' – produce some unfortunate effects; yet we might suggest that 'you cannot use the word "chiropodists" in an English poem: it would not be literary.' 'That is what is the matter with all the verse of to-day,' Ford wrote in January 1913, 'it is too much practised in temples and too little in motorbuses – LITERARY! LITERARY! Now that is the last thing that verse should ever be, for the moment a medium becomes literary it is remote from the life of the people, it is dulled, languishing, moribund and at last dead' (*LF* 54).

Songs From London, the title of Ford's 1910 volume, had brought together two vital strains in his poetic thought and practice. Many of his earlier poems are, as can be seen from other volume titles such as *Poems for Pictures and for Notes of Music*, or *The Question at the Well with Sundry Other Verses for Notes of Music*, 'lyric' in the literal sense. Ford's early intention to be a composer, his undoubted skill as a pianist and his substantial output of music and songs are, obviously, relevant.[37] And, whatever his misgivings about Rudyard Kipling, it is noticeable that Ford praises him not only for 'his boldness in the use of the vernacular' but also for 'his skill and his boldness ... in catching the rhythm of popular music, with its quaint and fascinating irregularities' (*CA* 177). It was of course with Kipling in mind that Ford described himself as 'for the banjo against the lyre all the time' (*CW* 29).

But of equal relevance is Ford's abiding concern, whichever the art he practised, with his reader or listener. And the second element in his title, 'From London', connects precisely with this concern for audience. Ford believed that the poets had lost ground to the novelists not only in the matter of diction, specifically 'the Poetic Vernacular' (*TR* 144) which made – which makes – so much nineteenth-century poetry so wearisome to read, but also in the relentless contraction of 'suitable' subjects for poetry. Ford knew that there is always an audience for 'romance', for the exotic, for that wholly removed, in time and space, from its readers' lives. But he believed that the primary audience which poets had to win back was that one which wished to read of recognizable things, places, people and situations, 'the poetry of cafés, of automobiles, of kisses, and of absinthe'.[38]

As we come up at Baker Street
Where tubes and trains and 'buses meet
There's a touch of fog and a touch of sleet;
And we go on up Hampstead Way
Towards the closing in of day ...

And again:

But here we are in the Finchley Road
With a drizzling rain and a skidding 'bus
And the twilight settling down on us.

And yet ... these are the first five and the last three lines of 'Finchley Road'. Between them lie twenty-four other lines of at least equal, though different, significance. Or rather, the opening and closing passages place reader and writer in the present of the writing while the rest of the poem is characteristic Fordian reverie, the mind elsewhere, the voices sounding in another time and place. In one of Ford's most familiar critical instances, Impressionism is suggested as serving:

> ... to render those queer effects of real life that are like so many views seen through bright glass – through glass so bright that whilst you perceive through it a landscape or a backyard, you are aware that, on its surface, it reflects a face of a person behind you. For the whole of life is really like that; we are almost always in one place with our minds somewhere quite other. (*CW* 41)[39]

It is often a matter not only of 'somewhere quite other' but 'some *time* quite other' also, Ford's tirelessly associative mind constantly inter-weaving and overlaying both temporal and spatial planes. Yet the shift into other times, into different but analogous situations, does not function simply as a setting of past against present: for all Ford's 'jeremiads' about the present and his celebrating of the past, of various pasts, he always begins from, and ends with, the acknowledgement of the present's primacy, and the absurdity of pretending otherwise. So, in

'The Three-Ten', the medieval world is evoked only to be set aside by the urgencies of his lovers' present:

But see, but see! The clock marks three above the Kilburn Station,
Those maids, thank God! are 'neath the sod and all their generation.

So, too, in the fine 'Modern Love', the battle between the two knights is powerfully rendered:

And one goes down among the emerald grass,
And one stands over him, his dagger poised,
His visor raised, his bloodshot eyes a-travel
Over the steel that lies between his feet,
Crushing the buttercups ... and so the point goes in
Between the gorget and the habergeon ...
And blood floods out upon the buttercups,
Gules, or and *vert* beneath an azure sky   (*CP1* 76)

It is rendered largely by the skilled insertion of the 'medieval' words into a colloquial, or at least, 'neutral' order of language. But the evocation of that world where 'in ten minutes it was win or lose' serves primarily to intensify the anticipation of 'all the long, long fight/That lies before us' (*CP1* 77).

Such ideas recur, of course, in Ford's novels: in *Ladies Whose Bright Eyes*, an historical romance which ends, as it begins, in the present, with a heightened sense of that present and of the need to go forward; in *Parade's End*, substantially an elegy for a gone world yet, equally significantly, a provisional mapping of a reconstructed one; and in *No Enemy*, avowedly 'A Reconstructionary Tale'.

The 'middle section' of 'Finchley Road' begins:

You should be a queen or a duchess rather,
Reigning in place of a warlike father
In peaceful times o'er a tiny town
Where all the roads wind up and down
From your little palace ...

'Should', 'you'd say', 'you'd set': not wish fulfilment but supposition, the poet's – or the novelist's – projection into other contexts and characters yet ('as your way is') with the present's 'visibility' always sustained. And the situation, in its essentials, is not an unachievable one in any present: the keying down of the ordinary processes of life, as Ford wanted to key down his prose;[40] conversation with the loved woman; a view, if not a 'great view'; and the writing, here of 'a little ode,/Part quaint, part sad, part serious ...'

The weaknesses of much of Ford's poetry are often traceable to rhyme:

> Down there where Europe's arms
> Stretch out to Africa

Good, though the political point in the pun registered by a modern reader was probably not in Ford's mind. Yet:

> Throughout the storms, throughout the calms
> Of centuries it took the alms
> Of sun and rain ... ('Two Frescoes. I. The Tower', *CP1* 128)

Is it unreasonable to cavil at 'alms'? Because the rhyme-word surely drags in its train the whole weak phrase 'it took the alms/Of sun and rain'. Ford used rhyme 'very frequently' as he himself noted:

> firstly because I like rhyme and vowel colourings in verse, and secondly because rhyme appears to have the effect of hastening verse along. I once wrote an immensely long poem in unrhymed Vers Libre – and it seemed immensely long and immensely wearisome! It was called *On Heaven*. I went through it again a month or so later and added rhymes to a great many lines. It at once seemed shorter and less wearisome. I fancy that the reason for this is that the mind, looking out for rhymes, hastens the tempo of its reading in order to achieve satisfaction. (*TR* 214-5)

Why 'hastening'? Ford recurs often, ironically yet surely with a profound seriousness, to his 'inability' to read poetry. But, if the moralizing comment and the 'poetic' language actually made so much of that poetry read so 'long', the sheer immensity of many Victorian works, reflecting a specific readership, social habits and cultural attitudes, the fact that those poems (and poets) 'went on and on – and on!' (*CW* 157), remained relevant. Ford found occasion to mention 'the thousand and a half odd pages of verse' (*PL* 191) which Swinburne had inflicted upon the world, as well as the 'endlessly returning metre' and the fact that Swinburne 'and his contemporaries' were 'already derivative', and that they 'supplied to the public of their unrhythmed day a facile substitute for the real classics ... as it were a piano version of orchestral masterpieces' (*PL* 201). Ford's legacy of weariness was, then, a substantive one, because many of his weakest poems suffer from his undoubted facility for rhyming, from a tendency to 'look about for a rhyme' (*CW* 161) and be led awry.

Still, rhyming or not, Ford is capable of great flexibility, not least between rhymed and unrhymed verse. 'Views' begins, with accurately abrupt and nervous 'units of sense',

> Being in Rome I wonder will you go
> Up to the Hill. But I forget the name ...
> Aventine? Pincio? No: I do not know.
> I was there yesterday and watched. You came.

And it continues:

> The seven Pillars of the Forum stand
> High, stained and pale 'neath the Italian heavens,
> Their capitals linked up form half a square;
> A grove of silver poplars spears the sky.   (*CPI* 71)

Yet the finest effects are both conversational and suggestive of that flickering instability at the edges of the writing: less a matter of the writer's control than of the writing's closeness to a mind in process, a mind characterized by a swift intelligence, by extensive resources, by a quickness of associative leaps:

> Just a glimmer of light there was across the grass
> And on my barrow mound. Upon his head
> The gleam of a helmet, and some sort of pelt
> About his shoulders and the loom of a spear.
> You never know these German regiments,
> The oddest uniforms they have; and as for her
> Her hair was all across her shoulders and her face,
> Woodland embraces bring the hairpins out ...
> ('To All the Dead': *CP1* 48)

'[A]nd as for her': the colloquialism gives the right touch, the potential awkwardness of 'her/Her hair' deflected not only by the line ending but by the assured sense of a voice talking: it is precisely the kind of awkwardness which the speaking voice does not bother itself about evading. And 'You never know these German regiments,/They have the oddest uniforms' – comment, yes, but not of a kind which disrupts the surface of the poem. Largely, again, because the careful choice of that single word, 'oddest', emphasizes once more the nature of the voice we hear. '[H]airpins', too, is exactly right, bringing the visual image vividly before the mind.[41] Such successes are local; the success of the poem as a whole derives precisely from that sense of a mind ranging, the swiftness of transit from the Chinese Queen to the room in the rue de la Paix to the American river to the German town, movements not only of place or time but of voice, of a complex variety of tone and modulation.

It is *voice*, almost always, that accounts for the successes of Ford's later poems, coming closest to his desired ideal in 'Buckshee':

> We shall have to give up watering the land
> Almost altogether.
> The maize must go.
> But the chilis and tomatoes may still have
> A little water. The gourds must go.
> We must begin to give a little to the mandarines

98

And the lemon-trees.

('L'Oubli–, Temps de Sécheresse': *CP2* 306)

And again:

I know you don't like Michaelangelo.
But the Universe is very large, having room
Within it for infinities of Gods
All co-existing, much as you and I
Drudge on, engrossed by paper or on canvas [...]   ('Coda': *CP2* 317)

If Ford does not consistently adhere to the poetic principles he proposes in his critical writings, he does, increasingly, vindicate his assertion that 'the main thing is the genuine love and the faithful rendering of the received impression' (*CP1* 28), that 'it is the duty of the poet to reflect his own day as it appears to him, as it has impressed itself upon him' (*CP1* 26). And Pound's late observation that Ford 'refused the Imagist rock-drill, intent on his own *donné*', sensibly emphasises that last phrase – 'his own'.[42]

Ford once observed of his *Collected Poems* that 'every single group of words was what in French is called *chargé*', alluding to his discovery that 'as soon as I came to write a "poem" I automatically reduced my intelligence to the level of one purely childish' (*TR* 132). That was his real Pre-Raphaelite inheritance, which he never wholly eluded: he could not treat poetry, certainly his own, with the same seriousness with which he treated prose, and, in that poetry, did not always remain the man who 'never dented an idea for a phrase's sake'.[43] Yet, if his poems are, in large part, the minor writings of a major writer, they frequently achieve something more than that. His earlier lyrics seem slight when they do not manage to impress upon us the music which ideally (and often literally) accompanied them; the poems of the early nineteen-tens are the most, and most fascinatingly, transitional, as Ford presents what were often, at that time, unfamiliar materials for poetry in an extensive variety of metrical forms; while the later poems, with some exceptions, are much closer to prose, though always exhibiting a marked awareness of the effects that rhyme, assonance and studied repetition can achieve or enhance. Along the way, Ford demonstrated, in *Mister Bosphorus and the Muses*, that he was capable of a peculiar, hybrid, more overtly 'modernist' work, or, as in *A House*, frankly pleased himself. Yet, in pleasing himself, Ford sought also to please 'the other person' in that long conversation. 'The justification of any method of art, the measure of its success, will be just the measure of its suitability for rendering the personality of the artist',[44] and, in most of Ford's work, certainly in much of the poetry, this is exactly the impression which the reader receives: that 'unaffected self' (*TR* 212); *humanitas*; a cultured, tolerant, and intensely human voice, 'a quiet voice going on talking and talking ... just quietly saying things'.

NOTES

1. This is only one version of those lines of a poem that Ford 'never published'. In their more frequent form, they refer to 'larger birds' (*TR* 213) or 'other birds' (*CA* 181; *BSDSG* 180; *CW* 156). The slippage from 'birds' to 'bards' recalls Ford's allusion to 'that brief moment when England had been a nest of singing birds' (*RY* 39). See also *JC* 11, where a robin makes a suggestive appearance, hopping across the kitchen floor 'between the waiting cats.'

2. *P/F*, 50-51.

3. Christopher Middleton, 'Documents on Imagism from the Papers of F. S. Flint', *The Review*, 15 (April 1965), 50.

4. *P/F*, 35-6.

5. F. S. Flint, 'The History of Imagism', *Egoist*, 2 (1 May 1915), 70-71; Middleton, 'Documents', 41. The salient verb recurs as late as Pound's note on Ford in *Confucius to Cummings*, New York: 1964, p. 327: 'the most important critical act of the half-century was in the limpidity of natural speech, *driven* towards the just word ...' (my emphasis).

6. See 'Ford Madox (Hueffer) Ford; Obit', in Pound's *Selected Prose*, edited by William

Cookson, London: Faber & Faber, 1973, pp. 431-2. Flint (like Ford) had served in the army: his military metaphors were perhaps intended to underline the fact that Pound had not, his 'war' being a quite different one.

7. See, particularly, Middleton, 'Documents', 39. See also John Gould Fletcher with the same grievance: *Life is my Song* (1937), New York: 1981, pp. 73-4. There is an excellent discussion of the contribution of the 'forgotten school' in Wallace Martin's *The New Age under Orage*, Manchester: 1967, Chapter IX, 'The Origins of Imagism'. See Pound's statement (dated August 1917) that he had written 'of certain French writers in *The New Age* in nineteen twelve or eleven', shifting that moment backwards in time: *Literary Essays*, edited by T. S. Eliot, London: Faber & Faber, 1960, p. 13. On Flint, see Le Roy C. Breunig, 'F. S. Flint, Imagism's "Maître d'Ecole"', *Comparative Literature*, 4:2 (Spring 1952), 118-36.

8. See Ford's 'The Making of Modern Verse', *Academy*, 62 (19 April 1902), 414; *Academy*, 62 (26 April 1902), 438. For the apparent date of composition, see Ford's letter to Olive Garnett, reprinted in *Reader*, pp. 466-7.

9. See Ford's review of Christina Rossetti's *Collected Poems*, in *Fortnightly Review*, 75 (1 March 1904), 397.

10. Ford, 'Literary Portraits: IV. Herr Gerhardt Hauptmann', *Tribune* (17 August 1907), 2.

11. See Ford, 'Literary Portraits: XXVII. Mr. Charles Doughty', *Tribune* (25 January 1908), 2.

12. *Ezra Pound and Dorothy Shakespear: Their Letters 1909-1914* edited by Omar Pound and A. Walton Litz, London: Faber & Faber, 1985, p. 155.

13. See also Ford's 'Literary Portraits: XXXIII. Mr Sturge Moore and "The Sea is Kind"', *Outlook*, 33(25 April 1914), 560. Cf. T. E. Hulme, writing approvingly – if somewhat ironically – in praise of processions: 'I regard processions as the highest form of art,' 'Notes on the Bologna Congress', *New Age*, 8, 26 (27 April 1911), 608. But see also Robert Hampson, '"Experiments in Modernity": Ford and Pound', in Andrew Gibson (ed.), *Pound in Multiple Perspective* (London: Macmillan, 1993), p. 121, n.31.

14. Ford, 'Literary Portraits: XIV. Mr. Maurice Hewlett', *Tribune* (26 October 1907), 2.

15. 'Literary Portraits: XXIII. The Year 1907', *Tribune* (28 December 1907), 2.

16. 'Publications Received', *English Review*, 4 (December 1909), 161.

17. William Wordsworth, *Poetical Works* (Oxford, 1969), p. 737. Ford's Wordsworthian affinities have been noted by Violet C. Skorina, 'Leaving "Wardour Street"' (Ph.D., University of Connecticut, 1979), 19, 88-9; Camilla Bunker Haase, 'Serious Artists: The Relationship Between Ford Madox Ford and Ezra Pound' (Ph.D., Harvard, 1984), 105; Joseph Wiesenfarth, 'The Ash-Bucket at Dawn: Ford's Art of Poetry', *Contemporary Literature*, 30, 2 (Summer 1989), 254; and cf. Hugh Kenner, 'The Poetics of Speech', in *Ford Madox Ford: Modern Judgements*, edited by Richard Cassell, London: Macmillan 1972, p. 179, on 'the documentary tradition'. For Ford on Wordsworth, see particularly 'The Making of Modern Verse: II', 438; *TR*, 14, 224; *ML*, 700-2.

18. Ford, 'Literary Portraits – XXXIX. Mr. W. B. Yeats and His New Poems', *Outlook*, 33 (6 June 1914), 783.

19. Ford, 'Pure Literature', edited by Max Saunders, *Agenda*, 27:4/28:1 (Winter 1989/Spring 1990), 5-22; quotation on p. 19.

20. Ford, 'Literary Portraits: XXXV.: Les Jeunes and "Des Imagistes"', *Outlook*, 33 (9 May 1914), 636.

21. Pound wrote to Harriet Monroe in April or May 1913: 'the question of "vers libre" is such old game. It's like quarrelling over impressionism or Manet.' Quoted by Ellen Williams, *Harriet Monroe and the Poetry Renaissance*, Urbana, Chicago and London: 1977, p. 50.

22. Ford, 'Les Jeunes and "Des Imagistes"', 653.

23. Ford, 'On a Notice of "Blast"', *Outlook*, 36 (31 July 1915), 144.

24. Ford, 'Les Jeunes and "Des Imagistes" (Second Notice)', *Outlook*, 33 (16 May 1914), 682.

25. See Ford, 'Literary Portraits – XLIV. Signor Marinetti, Mr. Lloyd George, St.Katherine, and Others', *Outlook*, 34 (11 July 1914), 46, 47.

26. Ford, 'Literary Portraits – XVII. Nineteen-Thirteen and the Futurists', *Outlook*, 33 (3 January 1914), 15. Cf. *MI*, 194, on the process of degeneration from Pre-Raphaelism to aestheticism to 'a sort of mawkish flapdoodle.'

27. D. I. B. Smith, 'Ford Madox Ford and Modernism', *University of Toronto Quarterly*, 51:1 (Fall 1981), 75-6.

28. Pound, 'The Prose Tradition in Verse', in *Literary Essays*, 374.

29. Ford, 'Les Jeunes and "Des Imagistes" (Second Notice)', 683.

30. And yet: see *GTR*, 165: 'the pilgrim fathers ... having given any sort of old country name to any sort of bird so that the robin is of the *turdus* family'.

31. Pound, *Gaudier-Brzeska* (New York, New Directions, 1970), p. 115.

32. See also *CW*, 156.

33. Ford, 'Les Jeunes and "Des Imagistes"', 653.

34. Pound, *Literary Essays*, p. 4.

35. 'Hugh Selwyn Mauberley: II', *Collected Shorter Poems* (Second Edition), London: Faber & Faber, 1968, p. 206. See Holbrook Jackson, *The Eighteen Nineties* (1913), Harmondsworth: Penguin, 1950, pp. 139, 142, on 'alabaster' as a 'Nineties' word.

36. Pound, *Literary Essays*, p. 5. Note Ford's comment that *Des Imagistes* contains 'an infinite amount of pure beauty – of *abstract* beauty' (my emphasis): 'Les Jeunes and "Des Imagistes"', 653.

37. See Sondra J. Stang and Carl Smith, '"Music for a While": Ford's Compositions for Voice and Piano', in *Contemporary Literature*, 30: 2 (Summer 1989), 183-223.

38. Ford, 'Mr Sturge Moore and "The Sea is Kind"', 560.

39. See also Ford, 'Literary Portraits – XXXI. Lord Dunsany and "Five Plays"', *Outlook*, 33 (11 April 1914), 495.

40. *TR* 52; see also *B* 44; *BSDSG* 56.

41. On hairpins, see Ford's Zola anecdote: *RY* 283, *ML* 772.

42. Pound, *Confucius to Cummings*, Norfolk, Connecticut: New Directions, 1964, p. 327.

43. Pound, 'Canto 82': *The Cantos of Ezra Pound*, London: Faber & Faber, 1975, p. 525.

44. Ford, 'Les Jeunes and "Des Imagistes" (Second Notice)', 683.

ENGLISH BEHAVIOUR AND REPRESSION:

A CALL: THE TALE OF TWO PASSIONS

Vincent J. Cheng

Ford Madox Ford's ideas about English repression and good behaviour, which he had earlier developed in *The Spirit of the People*[1] and which were to be so central to his acknowledged masterpieces *The Good Soldier* and *Parade's End*, were given their first novelistic treatment, not in *The Good Soldier* but, four years earlier, in *A Call*[2] – a novel which, in retrospect, seems almost a trial run for *The Good Soldier*. *The Spirit of the People* (1907) and *A Call* (1910) together suggest the composite picture of England and the English which Ford would try to depict in *The Good Soldier* (1915): a society admirable for its behaviour and good form but tragic in its consequent repression of emotions. This novel is, furthermore, a major and serious step by Ford in the development of not only the themes but also the techniques which he was to use in *The Good Soldier* and also in *Parade's End*, and which we have learned to characterize as 'Fordian'. While the novel is not as fully accomplished as *The Good Soldier* (although Ezra Pound thought it was[3]), yet in its sustained focus and concentration of action and character it shows all the promise that would blossom into the later novel.

A Call: The Tale of Two Passions bears fruitful comparison and parallels to *The Good Soldier: A Tale of Passion* in almost every way, starting with subtitles – for 'passion' is the key word of both novels. These subtitles to the two books are more revealing and appropriate than they may first appear, for, as also in *The Spirit of the People*, they are both studies of a society engaged in trying to repress its passions.

Although Ford acknowledged his debt to Henry James (there are a number of allusions to the novels of Henry James[4]) and although there are Jamesian qualities in both the novel's situations and dialogue, we can see in retrospect that *A Call* is not so much a Jamesian derivative as it is a Fordian development in novelistic technique, a trial run and exploration of the 'Impressionist' method and matter he would later employ to best effect in *The Good Soldier* and *Parade's End*.

Ford liked to describe his novelistic purpose as the depiction of an 'affair'. In the 'Epistolary Epilogue' to the novel, Ford explains that 'to me a novel is the history of an "affair"' (*Call* 299): in discussing the aims of 'your poor Impressionist', he elaborates further this conception of a novel:

> His [the Impressionist novelist's] sole ambition was to render a little episode – a small 'affair' affecting a little circle of people – exactly as it would have happened. (*Call* 304)[5]

In writing about *A Call*, Ford is referring specifically to the dance of his 'little circle' of four people – Robert Grimshaw, the woman he loves, his fiancée, and his best friend: 'four sparrows hopping delicately on their mysterious errands, ... going ironically through a set of lancers' (*Call* 18). In his very best novels we can further see just what Ford means by an 'affair': the inter-connected passions and emotions of a small circle of humans – illustrating, as it were, D. H. Lawrence's claim that 'the novel is the highest example of subtle inter-relatedness that man has discovered'.[6] *The Good Soldier* renders the subtle passions and dynamics, both overt and unspoken, between a 'four-square minuet' of 'good people'. *Parade's End* depicts, over a period of time and four separate novels, the emotions and conflicts between a 'small circle of people' – wife, lover, friend, brother – centred around Christopher Tietjens, the saga's hero. While *The Fifth Queen* trilogy has a much wider range of characters and a broad historical scope, nevertheless its story in Ford's hands ultimately also reduces to an 'affair' – the conflicting passions and ambitions of the triangle of Katharine Howard, Henry Tudor, and Thomas Cromwell. And it is significant that, in each of these major works, religion and religious beliefs are underlying influences on the human passions which compose the 'affair', playing a central role in determining character and story.

In both *A Call* and *The Good Soldier*, Ford combined the rendering of such an 'affair' with the typically Fordian narrative technique of *progression d'effet*, 'the slowly accelerated revelation of motive and meaning in a series of carefully dramatic scenes'.[7] As with *The Good Soldier*, the 'affair' in *A Call* affects a small 'minuet' of characters, four central characters forming a little circle of 'good people'; like *The Good Soldier*, its impressionistic *progression* contains time shifts and delayed revelations of crucial information. (But unlike *The Good Soldier*, the narrative viewpoint is third-person omniscient, thus avoiding the problems and ambiguities of narrator-reliability.) While it may be true, as some commentators have criticized,[8] that the story is based on a rather improbable premise (the wilful decision of Katya Lascarides, following her mother's example, not to be legally married), this flaw is noticeable only from a detached perspective and is not at all bothersome while the reader is engaged in the reading of the novel: after all, are not the situational premises of *The Good Soldier* equally implausible (Dowell's deception by Florence for twelve years, the two couples' sex-less married lives, the August 4 coincidences, and so on) yet equally accepted as the *données* of the 'affair' being rendered? Once the premises of *A Call* are accepted, the novel presents interesting characters engaged in delicate situations: as with *The Good Soldier*, the essence of the action is presented in specific, discrete scenes of dramatically revealing dialogue. Jointly, these form a strikingly Fordian impressionistic portrait of London society, following the portrayal of the English people Ford had painted in *The Soul of London*, *The Heart of the Country*, and *The Spirit of the People*. It is an engaging and successful piece of impressionistic novel-writing, and deserves to be recognized as such.

I

In *The Spirit of the People*, a book of non-fiction he wrote in 1907, Ford defined the relationship between Protestantism and English behaviour which he would increasingly depict in his novels. Protestantism, Ford wrote, 'availed itself of reason at the expense of intuition' (*SP* 115); the intuitive and the supernatural Ford associated with Catholicism. He argued that the English Revolution and Protestantism 'began that divorce of principle from life which ... has earned the English the title of a nation of hypocrites' and 'doomed England to be the land of impracticable ideals' (*SP* 81). Ford laments the loss in the Protestant religion of those instinctive, intuitive, non-rational elements that form the appeal and the authority of the Roman faith, that sense of humble faith in mysterious rituals, prayers, and divinity. Ford had just illustrated the power of these non-rational, even supernatural, elements of human faith in Papist Anne Jeal's power over Puritan Edward Colman in another novel, *The 'Half-Moon'*; he would champion such faith in mysteries and miracles while ridiculing over-intellectualized theology in *Mr Apollo* a year later.[9] In Ford's view, Protestantism has lost the simple faith in the divine (as opposed to human) powers which make religion comprehensible and viable to the average person; conversely, 'the whole being of great continental nations is imbued with a sense of the supernatural side of religion' (*SP* 118), a side of religion that England has lost.

These differences in the nature of the Protestant and Roman faiths are closely related in Ford's mind, indeed, with the issue of 'good form' versus openness of expression which would form the basis of his best-known novels. For, in Ford's mind, Protestantism, impractically based on the intellectual rather than the intuitive, helped bring about the denial of emotion and feelings which forms the basis of English 'good form' and self-repression; Catholicism, based as it is on the instinctual and supernatural, allows for greater openness and awareness of the emotional and the irrational. While Ford acknowledges that 'English manners were the best in the world' because of the English people's habit of 'repressing its emotions', yet 'we must set the fact that to the attaining of this standard [of manners] the Englishman has sacrificed the arts – which are concerned with expression of emotions – and his knowledge of life' (*SP* 151-52). Thus, significantly, religion and passions are linked to manners, national characteristics, and psychology.

To Ford, foreign Catholics have 'a sincerity that was entirely un-English' (*SP* 88), while English people, trained to good form through repression, are characterized by 'the singularly English faculty – the faculty of ignoring the most terrible of facts' (*SP* 92). His real-life illustration in *The Spirit of the People* is the germ incident which would grow into *The Good Soldier*: the stoic and silent parting between Edward and Nancy at the railway station, an example of the repression of emotion which Ford describes as 'a national characteristic that is almost appalling' (*SP* 151).

This inability to be open and honest with facts and feelings leads Ford to label Protestant England 'a nation of hypocrites' (*SP* 81). Saddled with a religion that encourages contemplation of the ideal and discourages being open about feelings and intuitions, the Englishman necessarily is dishonest with himself. For:

> ... the root fact is simply that the Englishman feels very deeply and reasons [openly about his feelings] very little. ... it is really because he is aware – subconsciously if you will – of the depth of his capacity to feel, that the Englishman takes refuge in his particular official optimism. He hides from himself the fact that there are in the world greed, poverty, hunger, lust or evil passions, simply because he knows that if he comes to think of them at all they will move him beyond bearing. He prefers, therefore, to say – and to hypnotise himself into believing – that the world is a very good – an all-good – place. (*SP* 145)

Thus, *The Good Soldier*'s 'good people' impose over their seething passions and instincts the form of an elegant minuet; thus *Parade's End*'s Christopher Tietjens tries to compose sonnets so that he need not think about his emotions. Such for Ford is the Englishman.[10]

II

As with *The Good Soldier*, the plot of *A Call* unravels as a dubious, Pyrrhic triumph of propriety over passion.[11] Its main character, Robert

Grimshaw, is the most clearly defined and depicted 'Fordian hero' in Ford's novels up to this point. Like Ford himself, Robert is half-English and half-foreign (Greek rather than German), brought up in the English public schools, and emotionally involved with two different women. Like both Dowell and Edward in *The Good Soldier*, he engages in the typical Fordian daydream of idealistic polygamy: 'I suppose what I really want is both Katya and Pauline' (*Call* 34); Etta Stackpole accuses him of wanting 'a little harem that doesn't go farther than the tea-table' (*Call* 169). More importantly, like other Fordian heroes (notably George Moffat, Edward Ashburnham, and Christopher Tietjens), Robert is imbued with a sense of public duty and propriety. Like *The Benefactor*'s George Moffat, he is committed to performing his duty and upholding his honour according to the moral code of his society, at the expense and denial of personal passion and feeling. Like George Moffat and Christopher Tietjens, he believes that 'some do not', and lives his life accordingly. Like Edward Ashburnham and Christopher Tietjens, Robert is English and Protestant and thus not privy – according to Ford – to the understanding and expression of passions/emotions. For, like Edward and Christopher and like the English/Protestant society Ford depicted in *The Spirit of the People*, he has been brought up to play the game and to be well-behaved – at the expense of understanding, or being able to deal openly with, his own emotions; it is a life of genteel 'traditions that are so infectious – of his English public-school training, of his all-smooth and suppressed contacts in English social life, all the easy amenities and all the facile sense of honour that is adapted only to the life of no strain, of no passions' (*Call* 281). This is what Ford sees as the English manners of good people: 'having been trained in the English code of manners never to express any emotion at all, he [Robert] had forgotten that he possessed emotions' (*Call* 282).

'Katya Lascarides,' Mizener points out, 'is a passionate, possessive, stubborn woman; as such, she is thoroughly convincing' (p. 480). Katya's profession is medical – she is an expert in 'the more obscure forms of nervous diseases' (*Call* 22) – but there is a singular, religious intensity about her being. Her rupture with her fiancé (Robert

Grimshaw) was 'generally thought to be due to religious differences' (*Call* 22); she is Greek Orthodox, he is Anglican. Going away to America after the rupture, she refuses to accept her proper inheritance from her late father, thus taking on 'some of the aspect of having become a nun, or, at any rate, of her having adopted a cloisteral [*sic*] frame of mind, devoting herself, as her sister Ellida said, "to good works"' (*Call* 23), curing nerve cases in America as if she were a missionary to the wilderness. As a healer, she is nothing short of phenomenal; her diagnostic miracles are the medical and constructive opposites to Anne Jeal's destructive black magic (in *The 'Half-Moon'*) and to Sylvia Tietjens's evil practices and trepannings (in *Parade's End*). Like Anne, Sylvia, and Leonora Ashburnham, Katya is Catholic (here, Greek Orthodox to suit the story's parameters), passionate, possessive, and obstinate; like all of them, her passion is manifest in the manipulative power she exercises over the man she loves, even if it does him harm or evil. Her cloistral obstinacy is like Leonora's connubial coldness to Edward, never giving in unless she gets her way: 'I have stuck to it [her decision not to marry Robert formally], and I will stick to it. Robert must give in, or I will never play the part of wife to him' (*Call* 105). Like Leonora (with her grip over Edward's finances), Katya is 'so professional, so practical, so determined' (*Call* 111).

Although Katya is similarly wilful and selfish, she is much more appealing than most of Ford's possessive, passionate female characters – such as the murderous Anne Jeal, the manipulative Sylvia Tietjens, or the vulgar Countess Macdonald in *The New Humpty-Dumpty* (1912). Her intelligence and her ability to face her feelings openly – in this she is un-English, according to Ford's vision of well-mannered English repression (that is, as a Continental 'Catholic' she knows and understands passion), and Ford describes her openly passionate character as a 'southern nature' (*Call* 23) – combine to make her attractively honest and self-aware. When, for example, she diagnoses the nervous condition of her young niece Kitty (who refuses to speak) – 'the desire to be made a fuss of, to occupy the *whole* mind of some person or of many persons, to cause one's power to be felt – are these motives not very human?' – she realizes that 'I am diagnosing my own case!' (*Call* 101). Katya's self-imposed exile to America, it is interesting to note, is, like Kitty's self-imposed muteness, a geographical if not literal commitment to silence, in order 'to cause one's power to be felt.' She realizes that, like Kitty's, her case is in fact 'a manifestation of passion ... of a disposition passionate in the extreme' (*Call* 103). Though Katya may fit the pattern of the Fordian villainess (like Anne Jeal, Sylvia, or even Leonora), her self-awareness, liveliness, and passionate nature make her, not only 'convincing' (as Mizener acknowledges), but positively and magnetically alive, in contrast to the effeminately bland and self-deceiving natures of the other characters in this story; in view of the English society depicted in *A Call*, Katya's palpable and vibrant reality provides an almost Lawrentian contrast with the Ricos and Chatterleys of the world. Significantly, Ford makes her (as opposed to the 'black witch' Anne Jeal) a white witch of sorts – 'engaged in good works' (*Call* 10) and healing sick people – never undercutting her with ridicule: she is not demeaned with the rapaciousness of Etta Stackpole, the murderousness of Anne Jeal, the vulgarity of Countess Macdonald, the promiscuity of Florence Hurlbird, or the sadism of Sylvia Tietjens.

Pauline Lucas, as a much younger Roman Catholic (*Call* 135) woman, is a grown-up and more sophisticated, more intelligent fore-runner of Nancy Rufford. She is self-controlled, thoroughly virtuous, quietly likable, and well-behaved in Ford's 'English' manner. Her husband Dudley Leicester, Robert's best friend, on the other hand, is a weak, vacillating, and nervously fragile hypochondriac. Although Mizener suggests that, as in *The Good Soldier* and in *Mr Fleight*, there is a doubling of the Fordian hero here into Robert and Dudley (p.262), in fact Dudley only has Dowell's non-heroic aspects, totally lacking Dowell's peculiar perceptiveness, humour, compassion, or sensitivity. Dudley seems to be more like a sickly puppy who is 'essentially innocent' (*Call* 68) and under the nurse-like care and direction of his wife – 'It's my task in life to keep him going,' she says; but 'he never realized that it was she who did it' (*Call* 127, 45). He can hardly be taken very seriously by the reader.

Robert, Katya, Dudley, Pauline: here we have the four-square minuet of this novel.[12] The story begins at Pauline's and Dudley's wedding, where Robert admits to Katya's sister Ellida that he has 'given [Dudley] what was dearest and best to me' (*Call* 14) – that is to say, Pauline. (It would be as if Edward Ashburnham actually married Nancy Rufford off to Dowell so as to keep himself honest!) What Robert thinks he feels for Pauline brings to mind what Edward claims to want from Nancy:

> ... tenderness, fidelity, pretty grace, quaintness, and above all, worship ... That's what I want in Pauline. I don't want to touch her ... Don't you see – just to watch her? She's a small, light bird. I want to have her in a cage ... and to have her peep up at me and worship me. (*Call* 17)

One recalls Edward's desire that 'the girl, five thousand miles away, should continue to love him' (*GS* 277-8)[13]. As Robert and Ellida 'stroll towards the Albert Memorial', they notice not one but four birds:

> He paused, indeed, to watch four sparrows hopping delicately on their mysterious errands, their heads erect through the grimy and long grass between the Park railings and the path. It appeared to him that they were going ironically through a set of lancers, and the smallest of them, a paler coloured hen, might have been Pauline Leicester. (*Call* 18)

Surely the other three, then, would be Robert, Dudley, and Katya. Here we have, in the sparrows dancing through a set of lancers, the theme of *The Good Soldier* immediately announced as that of *A Call*: the four-square minuet, the outwardly ordered and elegant dance of 'good people', performed by human beings who, as Mizener notes, 'try to move through its graceful figures ... with their uncontrollable passions, about as suited to it as these lustful sparrows' (p. 481).

What follows is a trial run for the railroad-station scene in *The Good Soldier*, the seed incident of which had previously been described in *The Spirit of the People*. For, just as Edward asks Dowell to accompany him to the station to see his beloved Nancy off (lest he be unable to maintain his rigid self-control), so also Robert begs Ellida to come with him to see Pauline and Dudley off, so that he, too, may maintain his composure and firmness of purpose; as he tells Ellida, 'I've arranged this marriage ... to keep myself for Katya,' and if Ellida doesn't accompany him to the station, 'I can't answer for what will happen if you're not there to safeguard Katya's interests' (*Call* 26). At the station, the goodbyes between Robert and Pauline are even more muted than Edward and Nancy's exchange of 'So long's (*GS* 288) – for no words pass at all between them: Ellida shakes Dudley's and Pauline's hands, while 'Grimshaw himself stood behind her [Ellida], his own hands behind his back' (*Call* 27); as the train glides out of the platform, they watch Pauline faint inside the train. Ford's own response after witnessing the silent parting between P—— and Miss W—— in *The Spirit of the People* was that 'a silence so utter, a so demonstrative lack of tenderness, seems to me to be a manifestation of a national characteristic that is almost appalling' (*SP* 151); Dowell's parallel response at the railroad station was to be similarly appalled: 'It was the most horrible performance I have ever seen' (*GS* 288). Similarly, in this exactly parallel train-parting scene in *A Call*, Ellida is horrified by the cold cruelty of such proper English behavior:

'Oh, Robert, ... what have you done it for? If she's so frightfully in love with you, and you're so frightfully in love with her ... and you've only got to look at her face to see. I never saw such misery. Isn't it horrible to think of them steaming away together?' (*Call* 29)

One might well ask Edward these same questions when he sends Nancy away to her hated father (Leonora says that 'in desiring that the girl should go five thousand miles away and yet continue to love him, Edward was a monster of selfishness' [*GS* 283]), in view of the suffering and madness which will follow:

'It's horrible,' Ellida repeated. 'You oughtn't to have done it. It's true I stand for Katya, but if you wanted that child so much and she wanted you so dreadfully, wasn't it your business to have made her happy, and yourself? If

I'd known, *I* shouldn't have stood in the way, not even for Katya's sake. She's no claim – none that can be set against a feeling like that.' (*Call* 30)

Ellida appeals to the primacy of passion and feelings, but Robert invokes propriety – 'What have we arrived at in our day and our class if we haven't learned to do what we want [read: what we *will*], to do what seems proper and expedient – and to take what we get for it?' (*Call* 30). He accuses Ellida of being 'sentimental' (Ellida, after all, has the same Greek 'southern nature' as her passionate sister): 'Oh sentimentality, sentimentality! I had to do what seemed best for, us all – that was what I wanted. Now I'm taking what I get for it' (*Call* 31). In his god-like manipulation of four people's lives for propriety's sake, Grimshaw may be willing to take what he gets – but he has no inkling, as the novel goes on to demonstrate, how strong passion really is and thus how painful will be what he and they all 'get for it'. As Ford argued in *The Spirit of the People*, the understanding and expression of passion/emotion seems available to the Continental/Catholic mind, but not to the repressed English/Protestant mentality, fixated by propriety. Here we have the central theme of both *The Spirit of the People* and *The Good Soldier* (as well as the latter's central germ incident) defining the basic conflict in *A Call*: the conflict between personal passion and public duty – the patina of the game one must play, the appearances and obligations one must stick to if society is to survive, the cock owed Aesculapius. As Robert says to Ellida, 'We're all – all of us, in our class and our day, doing the same thing. Every one of us really wants the moon, and we've somehow to get on with just the earth, and behave ourselves' (*Call* 34); 'Don't you understand,' he explains, 'that's how Society has to go on? It's the sort of thing that's got to happen to make us the civilized people that we are' (*Call* 33). Dowell will echo these words in *The Good Soldier*: 'these things have to be done; it is the cock that the whole of this society owes to Aesculapius' (*GS* 45). The game has to be played; but Ford won't let us forget the high price paid in suffering for behaving like 'the civilized people that we are'.

Here, then, is the essential idea of both *The Good Soldier* and *Parade's End*: the conflict between public responsibilities and personal passions, played out in the playing of the game. Robert Grimshaw's English/Protestant background leaves him unprepared to deal with passion or to understand emotions, and thus to 'know' himself or others.[14] Following the story's crucial phone call that gives the book its title, he gradually grows to understand the strength of his own and others' passions and suffering. As Mizener notes:

> The order and design imposed on life by the acceptance of responsibility is beautiful to him, though the sacrifice of people's real feelings it demands is destructive ... Passion is far stronger than he had been able to imagine when he decided to remain loyal to Katya and to make Pauline marry Dudley Leicester. (p.481)

Rather than either living with Katya on her terms, or marrying Pauline himself, Robert has doomed four people to unhappiness and suffering. He first realizes this after the focal phone call (the full details of which are revealed to the reader only late in the book) which forces him to face his true feelings about Pauline:

> ... at that moment Robert Grimshaw knew himself. He was revealed to himself for the first time by words over which he had no control. In this agony and this prickly sweat the traditions – traditions that are so infectious – of his English public-school training, of his all-smooth and suppressed contacts in English social life, all the easy amenities and all the facile sense of honour that is adapted only to the life of no strain, of no passions; all these habits were gone at this touch of torture ... When he had practically forced Dudley Leicester upon Pauline, he really had believed that you can marry a woman you love to your best friend without enduring all the tortures of jealousy. This sort of marriage of convenience that it was, was, he knew, the sort of thing that in their sort of life was frequent and successful enough, and having been trained in the English code of manners never to express any emotion at all, he had forgotten that he possessed emotions. Now he was up against it. (*Call* 281-2)

Once again, as in so many of Ford's novels before *The Good Soldier* – *Romance, The Fifth Queen, The 'Half-Moon', Mr Apollo, Ladies Whose Bright Eyes* – we find religion at the base of the plot. In *A Call*, the Fordian Roman Catholic position (which Ford had explained in the non-fiction, and which now he increasingly associated with Continental Catholicism) has been replaced by the Greek Orthodox Church in order to suit the story's details (Grimshaw is half-Greek, equivalent to Ford's German-Catholic half) concerning English people of Greek parentage. There is some discussion sprinkled throughout the novel about 'religious differences', which at first appear to be the ostensible cause of the rupture between Katya (who is Orthodox) and Robert (who is Anglican): 'Mrs Lascarides [Katya's mother] had been exceedingly attached to the Greek Orthodox Church, whereas, upon going to Winchester [along with Eton, the public school Ford himself most frequently claimed – falsely – to have attended], Robert Grimshaw, for the sake of convenience and with the consent of his uncle, had been received into the Church of England' (*Call* 22). Mr Held, the male nurse-attendant who helps Pauline take care of Dudley (who, after receiving the call, has become inexplicably mute and mad), is a Christian Scientist, and so there is also some discussion (mainly between Held and Ellida) about Christian Science and Mary Baker Eddy (e.g. *Call* 194-9, 236).[15] As it turns out, the basic plot-complication (that is, the original rupture between Katya and Robert) which creates the novel, does in fact stem, improbably or not, from a religious dilemma – from Mrs Lascarides's non-marriage (which Katya insists on emulating), which was apparently the result of the scarcity of Orthodox priests in England at the time to perform the ceremony. Katya explains:

'I've been inquiring even about the Orthodox priests there were in England at the time. There wasn't a single one! ... I dare say... she [Katya's mother] began to live with father without the rites of the Church because there was no Church she acknowledged to administer them.' (*Call* 120-1)

117

But, more importantly, there is a quasi-religious dimension and tenor to this novel, a sense of almost divine or supernatural power embodied within the human (as was literally the case in The 'Half-Moon' and Mr Apollo), the 'awesome holy' of the supernatural and irrational that Ford associated with Catholicism. Mr Held, the Christian Scientist, wants to become a 'Healer' (Call 235, and passim); but ironically the novel's real healer is Orthodox Katya, whose miracles of medical diagnosis make her, as a healer, seem like a combination of physician and magician. Although at times, like Anne Jeal, she is possessive, passionate, and selfish, she seems more like Mr Apollo performing his beneficial miracles than like Anne Jeal practising her destructive black magic.

Although Katya has returned from America with a record of and a reputation for such 'good works', her first 'miracle' in the novel's story is the curing of Ellida's daughter Kitty and her condition of obstinate silence (Katya had returned to England for that purpose at Ellida's request). The cure, significantly, is set off by her and Robert's physical passion for each other; as they embrace and kiss, Katya whispers:

> 'Oh, take me! Take me! Now! For good...'
> But these words that came from her without will or control ceased, and she had none to say of her own volition. There fell upon them the silent nirvana of passion.
> And suddenly, vibrantly, shrill, and interrupted by sobs and the grinding of minute teeth, there rose up in the child's voice the words: 'Nobody must be loved but me. Nobody must be loved but me.' (Call 113)

So it is a release of passion, of feeling and words 'that came ... without will or control' – the opposite of Robert's controlled 'English' repression – that is the catalyst for a healing miracle. Miraculously, the child speaks again. And it is a double healing, in a sense, because, as we have seen, it also allows Katya to diagnose herself and to gain self-knowledge (physician, heal thyself).

Dudley Leicester is also in need of healing, for the traumatic phone call he receives forms the crisis of complication in the plot by effecting in him a mental disorder marked by total silence; thus, one of the consequences of Robert's too proper behavior, as with Edward's in *The Good Soldier*, is to cause someone to go mad with suffering. Pauline and Robert, with the help of Mr Held and Ellida, play the game of appearances marvellously by treating Dudley in public as if everything were normal (and thus hiding his condition from London society), while covertly seeking the help of a leading psychiatrist (Sir William Wells), and finally, in desperation, of Katya. Katya then performs her second healing miracle. Dudley's condition of silence parallels that of Kitty, and both are 'healed' by Katya. Whereas Kitty's cure had been precipitated by a physical display of affection and passion between Katya and Robert, it is enough with the fragile and childishly innocent Dudley for some physical caresses and touching (an attention he presumably does not receive from his wife Pauline) to coax him out of his silence and begin his cure. This second miracle forms the climax of Part IV:

> Katya Lascarides approached, and, bending over him, touched with the tips of her fingers little and definite points on his temples and brows, touching them and retouching them as if she were fingering a rounded wind-instrument, and . . . when she asked: 'Doesn't that make your head feel better?' it seemed merely normal that his right hand should come up from the ceaseless drumming on the arm of the chair to touch her wrist, and that plaintively his voice should say: 'Much better; oh, much better!' (*Call* 266)

Dudley is miraculously able to speak again.[16]

Katya, then, is a physiological healer of nerve conditions. But for Robert Grimshaw's condition of repressed passion and behavior, Ford provides a spiritual healer, like Katya also a Greek Orthodox. This is the role played by the Orthodox priest whom Robert, in his repressed loneliness and confusion late in the book, meets on a park bench. They have a revealing conversation in which they discuss the issues behind Robert's attitudes towards human behaviour, and towards the repression of personal passion in favor of public duty and appearances; it is the priest who voices Ford's views (as presented earlier in *The Spirit of the People* and *Mr Apollo*) on this topic. As often in Ford's novels, the touchstone/spokesman of spiritual wisdom and truth is a priest (or god) – for example, Mr Apollo, Father Antonio in *Romance*, Father Consett in *Parade's End*.

This Orthodox priest, wearing his 'black cylindrical hat,' 'long black cassock' and 'the great beads of a wooden rosary' (*Call* 211), socratically and catechismally leads Robert to the novel's spiritual message. When he abruptly asks Robert, 'Tell me, my son . . . do we not, you and I, feel lonely in this place?' – Robert's answer exemplifies proper English behavior by ignoring actual personal feelings and truths, calling a spade a diamond: '"Well, it is a very good place," Robert Grimshaw said. "I think it is the best place in the world"' (*Call* 214). In *The Spirit of the People*, Ford had argued that it is this kind of avoidance and repression of realities that give the Englishman 'his particular official optimism' and cheeriness about everything: 'He prefers ... to hypnotise himself into believing – that the world is a very good – an all-good place' (*SP* 145). The priest suggests, on the contrary, that one should call a spade a spade: 'For I tell you that when we see this place to be lonely, then, indeed, we see the truth, and when we say that it is pleasant, we lie foully' (*Call* 215). Here is the lesson Dowell learns in *The Good Soldier* about the minuet that is really a prison, the goodly apple rotten at the core. Grimshaw follows up this revelation by suggesting the implications and consequences of the priest's advice: '"Then indeed," Robert Grimshaw said, "we ... are to be creatures of two natures. We shall follow our passions"' – even if '"they lead us, as always they must, into evil"' (*Call* 216). The priest agrees, pointing out that 'we must purge then from us that satisfaction of well-doing and well-being by abstentions and by fastings' (*Call* 216) – which accurately describes the life Robert has led in denying his passions for the sake of 'well-doing' and propriety. A bit later Grimshaw voices his qualm more directly: 'So that we should not think too much of the effects of our deeds?' 'Not too much,' the priest answers, and tells Robert an anecdote about a woman who told her niece: '"My dear, never keep a diary; it may be used against you!" The priest pronounced these words with a singular mixture of laughter and contempt. "Do you not hear all England speaking in these words?" he asked suddenly' (*Call* 217-8). Ford here underscores the absurdity of good English behaviour in the cause of public reputation and appearances, the unnaturalness and dishonesty of the aloof and 'proper' shielding of one's eyes from emotional truth. "'The English", the priest diagnoses, "are always afraid of entanglements – that it may be used against them' (*Call* 221). Grimshaw now restates and repeats the doctrine he is being taught: 'Then you don't advise me ... to pull up my sticks – to wash my hands of things and people and affections?' The priest answers by urging him not to be afraid of affections and emotions: "'Assuredly," the priest said, "I do not advise you to give away your little dog for fear that one day it will die and rend your heart"' (*Call* 221). In declining Robert's proffered arm to lean on in walking back to his church, the priest ironically reminds him: 'but all other human contacts lie open to you. Cherish them' (*Call* 222). The discussion of Robert's behaviour and of the priest's advice – to be more of a man of feelings and not of aloof British reserve – is over, and has resembled nothing if not a Catholic confession. The priest ends by delivering his forgiveness, absolution, and penance, which Robert accepts:

> 'Go out into the world; help all that you may; induce all that you may to go into the right paths. Bring one unto the other, the mutual comprehension may result. That is the way of Christian fellowship; that is the way to bring about the peace of God on earth.'
> 'And pray God to forgive any ill that I may do,' Grimshaw answered.
> 'That, too,' the priest answered ... (*Call* 222-3)

Robert Grimshaw has received his spiritual absolution and healing.[17]

And so we have in the novel two Orthodox healers – a physical healer and a spiritual healer, a doctor and a priest.[18] Both – one by example and one by teaching – exemplify the antithesis of the English (and Anglican) public-school life of 'no strain, of no passions' which Robert Grimshaw has heretofore led.

III

Meanwhile, as in *The Good Soldier*, our four-square minuet of 'good people' have been trying to live their elegant English life, a life put to the test by the crisis of the call Dudley received and which drives him mad and silent. In the face of this crisis, Pauline plays the game best of all – and her behaviour forecasts the marvellous British aplomb of the Ashburnhams in the face of the realities behind their apparently perfect marriage – by keeping up 'the pretence that Dudley Leicester was ... an engrossed politician' (*Call* 200) and thus given to eccentric behaviour; even Robert wonders 'For how long could Pauline keep it up?' (*Call* 200). Again and again, she manages to maintain appearances in public, in social engagements, keeping everyone outside of the immediate circle from the truth about Dudley's condition, leading Ellida to remark: 'Oh, she's saved the situation again! ... Oh, isn't she wonderful!' (*Call* 202-3), while Pauline, 'with her brown eyes a little averted, ... without any visible emotion,' maintains the charming facade of the perfectly happy hostess, even to Ellida: 'And how is your little Kitty? She is still at Brighton with Miss Lascarides? Robert dear, just ring the bell for the tea-things to be taken away' (*Call* 204). Pauline is a frighteningly tragic vision of a hyperborean English sensibility who plays the game too well, 'fend[ing] off these approaches [of feeling and sympathy from Ellida's "southern nature"] by the attentive convention of her manner' (*Call* 205). Observing all of this, Robert, who himself has always acted under similar restraints, understands Pauline's behavior:

> They were in the face of Dudley Leicester's condition; they had him under their eyes, but Pauline was not going – even to the extent of accepting Ellida's tenderness – to acknowledge that there was any condition about Dudley Leicester at all ... Pauline was not going to show either gratitude or emotion for the moment. It was her way of keeping her flag flying ... 'Perhaps,' he thought to himself, 'until she knows it's hopeless, she's not going to acknowledge even to herself that there's anything the matter at all.' (*Call* 205-6)

Ford's vision of English behaviour, exemplified here by Pauline, is at once nobly tragic, sympathetic, and pathetic: 'an incessant vigilance, a fierce determination to keep her end up, and to do it in silence and loneliness' (*Call* 210-11).

Pauline and Robert, two of a kind, at least can be honest with each other as they grow to realize the dungeon of suffering they have entombed themselves into. Her description of her lonely life 'keeping her end up' is as heartbreaking as that of Charlotte Verver's final fate in James's *The Golden Bowl*:

> 'Don't you understand? Not only because it isn't delicate or it doesn't seem the right thing to talk about one's relations with one's husband, but simply ... I can't. I can keep things going; I can run the house and keep it all dark... I can *do* things. It drives me mad to have to think about them. And I've no one to talk to, not a relation, not a soul in the world.' (*Call* 228-9)

Grimshaw, realizing all the suffering he has caused, can only ask, 'You aren't angry with me?' But Pauline understands the course they have committed themselves to, revealing a more clear-sighted awareness of their mutual emotions than Robert has heretofore had: "'It's no use hiding our heads in the sand," she said, and then she added in cold and precise words: "You're in love with me and I'm in love with you. We're drifting, drifting. But I'm not the woman to drift. I mean to do what's right, and I mean to make you. There's no more to be said"' (*Call* 230). As with Edward's decision to send Nancy away in *The Good Soldier* (and as with Maggie Verver's and Charlotte's dilemmas in *The Golden Bowl*), Robert and Pauline have sentenced themselves to a life of propriety and pain.

By this point, Robert has had his conversion/encounter with the Greek Orthodox priest. Racked by the pains and passions of his involvement with two women, he – like Edward being flayed alive by Leonora and Nancy at Branshaw Teleragh, and like Ford in his marital dilemmas with Elsie and Violet – now desires only rest and 'the peace of God':

'The peace of God,' Robert Grimshaw said ... 'The peace of God, which passeth all understanding ... I've always thought that those words, coming where they do, are the most beautiful thing in any rite ... I just give in. I just want ... the peace of God.' (*Call* 250, 260)[19]

Finally, after Dudley has been miraculously healed by Katya – and thus his marriage with Pauline has been viably reaffirmed and sealed – Robert and Pauline, in the novel's final conversation between them, both realize the lesson (too late to do them any good) taught by the priest. For, unlike Katya, who had – with 'the determination of a tiger' (*Call* 260) – run her life according to her passions, the two of them, as 'good people', had not. They realize that 'in any case Katya [with her Greek "southern nature"] isn't of our day or our class' (*Call* 272). But now Pauline acknowledges their error in having ignored their feelings for each other:

'Robert,' she said gravely, '... Why are your hands shaking like that, or why did I just now call you "my dear"? We've got to face the fact that I called you "my dear"... I haven't made a scandal or an outcry about Dudley Leicester. That's our day and that's our class. But look at all the difference it's made in our personal relations! Look at the misery of it all! That's it. We can make a day and a class and rules for them, but we can't keep any of the rules except just the gross ones like not making scandals ... And that's the best that's to be said for us. We haven't learned wisdom: we've only learned how to behave. We cannot avoid tragedies.' (*Call* 272-4)

Her words are painful and powerfully poignant. Similarly, in 'the misery of it all' in *The Good Soldier*, Edward and Nancy and Leonora, in observing the rules and playing the game, have not been able to avoid tragedies – have only learned how to behave. Is good behaviour enough of an ethic to live by? *The Good Soldier*'s final images – of Edward about to kill himself with a penknife and of a mad Nancy, still behaving properly while uttering 'Shuttlecocks!' (*GS* 290) – encapsulate imagistically what Pauline has rendered verbally here: the purely

Pyrrhic victory gained by maintaining the proper behaviour of 'good people' in 'our day and our class'. What is left at the end, as in *The Golden Bowl*, is tragic indeed – two unhappy marriages (for Katya does finally marry Robert); as Pauline tells Robert, 'You do not love Katya Lascarides: you are as cold to her as a stone. You love me, and you have ruined all our lives. But it doesn't end, it goes on' (*Call* 275). Like Edward in *The Good Soldier*, Robert has indeed ruined all their lives – and sentenced them to living hell. Such are the wages of repression and propriety.

IV

As all Ford's novels show, Ford certainly did admire the bonds of public duty, responsibility, and seemliness pursued in the game of appearances by English 'good people' – and in his own life would claim Robert Grimshaw's English/Protestant public-school background as his own. Surely Ford in part admired the nobility of both Pauline's and Robert's intentions – just as he admired Edward and Nancy in *The Good Soldier*. And surely Ford in part did, like Dowell, feel threatened by the loss of such spirits, and in turn threatened by the manipulative passions and jealousies of the Leonoras and Katyas of the world. In fact, in the 'Epistolary Epilogue' to *A Call*, Ford goes as far as to admit that 'personally I extremely dislike' Katya Lascarides (*Call* 301). Yet towards Katya, as towards so many issues, the evidence shows that Ford in fact had very mixed feelings – as he did towards Anne Jeal, towards Leonora Ashburnham, towards Elsie Hueffer. In Katya he has painted a portrayal of an efficiently effective, possessive, and passionate nature, who is capable of performing constructive and healing miracles, and who, in her 'Catholic', Continental self-knowledge and openly passionate nature, does not need to repress her emotions and so refuses to play the game of English 'good people' which Ford similarly partly admires and partly decries.

For it is *that* that is the crux of Ford's ambivalence about all the dancers of these two minuets, *A Call* and *The Good Soldier*. As a result, his feelings for Robert Grimshaw – who, along with Pauline, is the embodiment of the game one must play 'to keep their end up' – are similarly mixed. Mizener reminds us that 'Ford clearly means us to admire this attitude' of public responsibility (p. 481); this is in part true. But in the 'Epistolary Epilogue' Ford's comments more accurately reflect, as does the novel itself, his ambivalence when he describes Robert Grimshaw as 'an amiable but meddlesome and inwardly conceited fool ... pathetically or even tragically, reaping the harvest of his folly" (*Call* 301). And lest readers mistake his intentions (as they would do with *The Good Soldier*), he admits explicitly:

> But when I found that ... moderately sane persons who had read the book [*A Call*] in its original form failed entirely to appreciate what to me has appeared as plain as a pikestaff – namely, that Mr. Grimshaw was extremely in love with Pauline Leicester, and that, in the first place, by marrying her to Dudley Leicester, and, in the second place, by succumbing to a disagreeable personality [presumably Katya], he was committing the final folly of this particular affair – when I realized that these things were not plain, I hastened to add ... passages of explicit conversation. (*Call* 302)

Ford did not provide similarly explicit comments about *The Good Soldier*, and that book has consequently spawned much confusion among readers about Ford's attitude towards his characters. In *A Call* we clearly see that Ford simultaneously admired the noble intentions in Robert Grimshaw's sense of public responsibility and decorum – but was also simultaneously appalled by its coldness, its emotional dishonesty, and the legacy of suffering it leaves behind. These were the qualities of the English-Protestant mind (also inherited by English Catholics with their rigid Non-conformist consciences) that Ford had already elaborated in *The Spirit of the People*.

In direct contrast, the intuitive and openly emotional mind of the Continental Catholic – as also described in the non-fiction and as represented here by two Greek Orthodox characters, the nun-like physician Katya and the priest – are able to express their emotions openly and have consequent self-knowledge within that 'mysterious, sub-rational realm of men's under selves and the powers that operate there' (Mizener 478). As a result, they are able to perform healing miracles. Furthermore, Katya's physiological healing arises out of her ability to be in touch with physical passions – while the priest is given the role of Fordian spokesman in pointing out the hypocrisy and suffering caused by not being in touch with one's passions, by the emotional repression bred in the Anglican public-school mentality.

We have seen, then, that *The Spirit of the People* and *A Call* both deal with the basic theme of *The Good Soldier* – and that they help clarify Ford's authorial stance in that later novel. *A Call* makes its position more clearly than *The Good Soldier*, not only because it has an explicit author's epilogue defining Ford's attitudes, but also because its narrator is omniscient – and thus the novel avoids the ambiguity and confusions of interpretation which result from the narrative opinions of an arguably unreliable narrator like Dowell. These same stances are, furthermore, corroborated by Ford's non-fiction work three years earlier, *The Spirit of the People*. Looking at these three books in conjunction, we can see their similarities, patterns, and parallel development of ideas and attitudes. In this light, many of Ford's novels (including the *Parade's End* tetralogy) can be seen as a collective critique and condemnation of English repression of feelings, of what Ford sees as the result of Anglo-Saxon Protestantism and 'English public-school training ... adapted only to the life of no strain, of no passions" (*Call* 281). Such a perspective helps us clarify Ford's own attitudes in *The Good Soldier*: Dowell's lament over the passing of an age of noble spirits (such as Edward and Nancy) must be qualified by Ford's mixed feelings – as Dowell himself says, 'I think it would have been better in the eyes of God if they had all attempted to gouge out each other's eyes with carving knives. But they were "good people"' (*GS* 286) – and by the three books' clear criticism of British reserve and the repression of feelings, of playing the game coolly with a stiff upper lip while being unable to face or understand one's own passions and feelings. Such behaviour may provide a superficially elegant and pleasing patina of order and propriety, but results 'pathetically or even tragically', in 'reaping the harvest of [their] folly' (*Call* 301) – a harvest of suffering, madness, and suicide. As Ford commented (in *The Spirit of the People*) on recalling his friend P——'s expressionless parting with Miss W—— at the railway station, knowing (in retrospect) that she would die 'at Brindisi on the way out' and that P—— would spend the next years 'at various places on the Continent where nerve cures are attempted':

> [I]t was playing the game to the bitter end ... But a silence so utter, a so demonstrative lack of tenderness, seems to me to be a manifestation of a national characteristic that is almost appalling. (*SP* 150-1)[20]

NOTES

1. *The Spirit of the People: An Analysis of the English Mind*, London: Alston Rivers, 1907.

2. *A Call: The Tale of Two Passions*, London: Chatto & Windus, 1910, hereafter abbreviated in citations to *Call*; all quotations and page citations are from this edition. The novel has since been reprinted in editions by Carcanet and by Ecco Press.

3. In a letter to Pound's father on September 12, 1923; see Bernard J. Poli, *Ford Madox Ford and the Transatlantic Review*, Syracuse: Syracuse University Press, 1967, p. 19.

4. For example, we find the names Moddle (from *What Maisie Knew*), Brigstock (from *The Spoils of Poynton*), and Etta Stackpole (versus Henrietta Stackpole in *The Portrait of a Lady*).

5. Ford also defined, in *The Critical Attitude*, London: Duckworth, 1911, this concept of the novel as one practised by James and Conrad: 'Each takes in hand an "affair" – a parcel of life, that is to say, in which several human beings are involved – and each having taken hold never loosens his grip until all that can possibly be extracted from the human situation is squeezed out' (p. 89).

6. Lawrence, 'Morality and the Novel' (1925). Reprinted in D. H. Lawrence, *Selected*

Literary Criticism, ed. Anthony Beal, New York: Viking, 1966, p. 110.

7. This succinct definition is Mizener's: Arthur Mizener, *The Saddest Story: A Biography of Ford Madox Ford*, New York: World Publishing, 1971, p. 478, hereafter cited as Mizener. Mizener also notes the connection between the two novels in terms of technique: 'In *The Good Soldier*, Ford made, for the first time, a success of the method of narration that was to be peculiarly his own, toward which he had been struggling in novels like *A Call* – 'the first of Ford's novels that is explicitly "An Affair" with Ford's typical *progression d'effet'* (pp. 255, 478).

8. For example, Mizener, pp. 199, 479-80; Carol Ohmann, *Ford Madox Ford: From Apprentice to Craftsman*, Middletown, CT: Wesleyan Univ. Press, 1964, pp. 54-6.

9. *The 'Half-Moon'*, New York: Doubleday, 1909; *Mr Apollo*, London: Methuen, 1908.

10. The above four paragraphs, summarizing Ford's depiction of English society in *The Spirit of the People*, are adapted from an earlier essay of mine more fully investigating the nature of English repression in both *The Good Soldier* and *The Spirit of the People*. Vincent J. Cheng, 'The Spirit of *The Good Soldier* and *The Spirit of the People*', *English Literature in Transition 1880-1920*, 32:3 (Fall 1989), 303-16.

11. Mizener provides a brief plot summary (p. 479).

12. There are also several interesting minor characters, foremost of whom is Etta Stackpole, who in her sexual rapaciousness and vulgarity is a forerunner of Florence Hurlbird: 'she had all the wilfulness of an only daughter, and all the desperate acquisitiveness of the Elizabethan freebooters from whom she was descended' (*Call* 53); she tells Dudley that 'I've always wanted men about me, and I mean to have them ... The world has got to give me what I want, for it can't get on without me' (*Call* 66). In her claim that she is a 'religious woman' who 'believe[s] in angels and the devil' (*Call* 182, 177) but who nevertheless performs her sexual trepannings, she is also a bit like Sylvia Tietjens.

13. Citations from *The Good Soldier* are taken from the World's Classics edition, ed. Thomas C. Moser, Oxford: Oxford University Press, 1990.

14. In this he is rather like Dowell; what Robert realizes about one's limited knowledge of people is what Dowell will discover when he finds he doesn't 'know' the Ashburnhams or Florence at all: 'But we never can and we never shall know what anyone in the world knows of us and thinks. You'll find, as you go on, that you'll never really know *all* that Pauline thinks of you – not quite all. I shall never really know all that you think about me. I suppose we're as intimate as men can be in this world, aren't we? Well!' (*Call*

86).

15. In *The Spirit of the People* Ford had written that 'the church founded by Mrs. Eddy is the first modern faith to be evolved by a woman' and suggests that women 'must found the religions of the future' (*SP* 107, 111). In *Ladies Whose Bright Eyes*, written a year later, Mr Sorrell makes passing references to Christian Science (Philadelphia: Lippincott, 1935), pp. 83, 98.

16. It is curious to note the repeated pattern of neurological or self-imposed muteness in Ford's novels: Kitty, Katya (her self-imposed silence of exile), Dudley, and *Last Post*'s Mark Tietjens – all of whom get somehow cured.

17. The priest's words – perhaps even the priest's elderly, bearded appearance – may have been based on Ford Madox Brown, for in the tribute he wrote a year later for his famous grandfather, Ford recalls Brown continually enjoining him when he was young, as Ford also now was enjoining his daughters, 'to act then upon the lines of your generous emotions, even though your generous emotions may at the time appear to lead you to disaster' (*Memories and Impressions: A Study in Atmospheres*, New York: Harper, 1911, xv).

18. In contrast, the 'healer' prized by London society, the highly respected nerve-doctor Sir William Wells, is portrayed as an arrogant and ineffective quack, failing miserably in trying to cure Dudley; this is perhaps Ford's comment on modern psychiatry and all the modern cures – 'soda-water douches, pork-and-ice cream diets, and indecent photographs'! – that the latest German nerve specialists in Mammern or Marienberg tried on Ford in an attempt to cure him of his agoraphobia and nervous breakdowns. See Mizener, Chapter 9 on these German quackeries.

19. Mizener discusses how at this time Ford 'was an uncertain and unhappy man, longing for tenderness and "rest"' (p. 174). The 'peace of God, which passeth all understanding' is discussed by Ford in *SP*, 91-2, and by Dowell *GS* 288. Edward's last words are: 'So long, old man, I must have a bit of rest, you know' (*GS* 294).

20. In his 1913 study of *Henry James*, London: Martin Secker, 1913; reprinted New York: Octagon Books, 1964, written at the same time as *The Good Soldier*, Ford would again note that, while the Anglo-Saxon Protestant 'is incapable of calling a spade and spade' (*sic*) and 'shrinks from the definite statement', on the other hand 'the Latin and the Papist spirit isn't in the least afraid of definition'. Ford then warns that this British repression of emotional realities may be the 'destined and ultimate cause of the downfall of the Anglo-Saxon empires, since the race that cannot either in allegories or in direct speech think clearly is doomed to fall before nations who can' (*HJ* 92, 170-2). 'In such a context,' as I have argued, 'the England of Ford's novels acquires the poignant

perspective of a race tragically and hypocritically committed to the facade of good form and emotional repression, ignoring the realm and truths of the intuitive and the passionate.' Cheng, 'The Spirit of *The Good Soldier* and *The Spirit of the People*, p. 315.

THE MARSDEN CASE

AND THE TREATMENT OF READING

Max Saunders

Rumours of Ford's neglect have been exaggerated. His best and best-known novels, *The Good Soldier* and *Parade's End*, have been fairly continuously in print in either Britain or America since the Second World War; *The Fifth Queen* trilogy since the 1960s. He has never lacked eminent champions. But his other works have been more problematic, and it is the problem of their neglect that this volume squarely confronts.

There are doubtless many reasons: changes in literary and critical fashions that have moved the spotlights away from dead white European male authors; Ford's investment in a genre which for a long time seemed unreadably dated – historical romance – but which post-modernism has now reanimated; possibly even his sheer versatility – the disconcerting unlikeness of so many of his works from each other, or from anyone else's books.

There is also a specific problem which has troubled me while reading some of his less well-known fiction of contemporary life. This is that Ford draws upon his own experiences of the literary life – as many writers do – but that he wants to attach to those experiences a more universal and apocalyptic significance than they will bear. I shall argue that this critical problem can yield a new approach to Ford's prose.

Mr. Fleight, to take a pre-war example, is in many ways a vivid and compelling novel. But its rendering of Edwardian social and political life seems to me restricted by Ford's wanting to use his own experience of founding and losing the *English Review* as somehow representative of a general hypocrisy and corruption. Ezra Pound said that appreciation of Ford's social satires was 'difficult for those not in eng. at least from 1908-20', and that works like *Mr. Fleight* and *The Simple Life Limited* were:

both in surface technique, presumably brilliant, and but for levity, wd. be recognized as hist. docs. are so recog. by those who know how close their apparent fantasia was to the utter imbecilities of milieu they portray. Unbelieved because the sober foreigner has no mean of knowing how far they corresponded to an external reality.[1]

The hysteria and social turmoil they portray are indeed corroborated by other kinds of historical document, such as George Dangerfield's classic *The Strange Death of Liberal England*. From another point of view, perhaps Ford's 'fantasia' isn't fantastical enough, but remains too grounded in something too specific to himself: not just the small world of literary magazine publishing, but the extremely small world of his own anarchic-altruistic version of it.

Similarly, in an unpublished post-war novel, variously titled 'That Same Poor Man', 'The Wheels of the Plough', and 'Mr Croyd', the protagonist, Jethro Croyd, is a great writer, not merely neglected, but vilified, betrayed, and conspired against by the literary establishment. 'I am just finishing a novel about La Vie Litteraire', Ford told Pound in 1920: 'It is turning out rather finely macabre.' The finishing proved hard to finish, though. 'It is turning into an Immensity – a sort of Literary Via Dolorosa. . . . I viewed it with suspicion at first; but it comes on', he told Pound three days later. It was another three months before it was ready to send to his agent, J. B. Pinker.[2] He gave it a thorough revision in 1928. But it wasn't published then, nor in 1939, when his British publisher Stanley Unwin was considering it. Some parts are extremely good; in particular, the raw psychological accounts of Croyd's war experiences and their aftermath.[3] Yet Ford was right, I think, to view it 'with suspicion'. In a way, Croyd's persecution anticipates that of Tietjens in *Parade's End*. The wartime sufferings of both men are seen as the direct result of their pre-war persecutions – by Society and his Society wife Sylvia, in Tietjens' case; by literary society in Croyd's. By the time he began *Parade's End* Ford had perhaps attained enough distance from his own feelings of social and literary ostracism to be able to represent it in broader, more complex terms. So although individual vindictivenesses are very vivid – indeed Sylvia's is problematically so for a reading informed by feminism – the work as a whole doesn't blame the war entirely on marital troubles, or on women, or on the Civil Service which employs Tietjens, or on any individual or group alone. Rather, one can see *Parade's End* as a kind of *Anatomy of Human Destructiveness* (to use Erich Fromm's phrase), exploring precisely where human violence originates, and finding that it is everywhere and in everyone. Yet Ford's presentation of the literary enmities surrounding Jethro Croyd doesn't quite have this wider relevance. Perhaps the problem lay in Ford's contradictory aims for the book: to satirise 'La Vie Litteraire', and thus undermine the pretensions of the literati, on the one hand; but on the other, to glorify the sufferings of the same literary life: to write 'a sort of Literary Via Dolorosa'.

I

It is to the next novel Ford wrote that I wish to turn for the rest of this essay: *The Marsden Case*. It too seems to me almost a brilliant novel, but one compromised by the same problem of the relationship between the protagonist and his social context. The protagonist, George Heimann, is not a writer. He is an aristocrat, whose sufferings (social persecution and familial anxiety) are juxtaposed with the more general suffering caused by the war. Heimann has been seen as another precursor of Tietjens. But *The Marsden* Case scarcely treats of the Western Front. The novel forms a diptych, with the war falling between the two halves. This tends to produce the effect noted by Robert Green, when he says: 'there is a strange lack of connection between the public events and the suffering hero'.[4] Criticism of this kind of problem in Ford has tended to be grounded in terms of either character or society. Arthur Mizener argued that Tietjens was 'like all Ford's characters, not strictly realistic'.[5] From a Marxist point of view, such as that of Robert Green's book, fiction needs to be 'validated' by social realities of class and history.

Such comments tell us much about Ford's writing. Like Flaubert, and many other great writers, Ford was indeed engaged in something other than strict realism: something he called 'Impressionism'. And he was always interested in characters disconnected in some way from their time and place: people living against the grain of their society, struggling against the current of their situation. In themselves neither criticism would necessitate a negative judgement. But I don't dissent from the view that there is something about *The Marsden Case* that doesn't quite work. In part, as I have argued elsewhere, it is that the juxtaposition of George's near-suicide and the war backfires: that instead of amplifying the pathos of George's case, the background of the war trivializes it.[6] But also – and this is the point I want to pursue here – it is too literary. Of course writers can write about, and write well about, writing. It is again a problem of connection. As in *Mr Fleight* and 'Mr Croyd', the juxtaposition of literary squabbles with social and national conflicts makes us take the literary plots less seriously, not more.

However, the critical interest of this problem is much greater. In the rest of this essay, I want to turn it around, to ask why Ford involves literature as a subject in so many of his novels; and to ask what this can tell us about his writing in general – not just those novels, but also his better-known and more highly-regarded ones; and also his critical and reminiscential prose. I hope to be able to show that what proves problematic in some novels helps to account for the strength of others, and other forms. His literariness, that is, can also be seen as part of a critical exploration of the nature of literature, and especially of the experience of reading. Finally I shall argue that Ford's ways of figuring the experience of reading might also tell us something about the nature of Modernism, and of his significance for it.

In an earlier discussion of *The Marsden Case* I have written about its concern with writing, reconstruction, and psychology.[7] Here I shall concentrate on the way reading figures in the book; but as this is often inextricable from the other terms, first I shall briefly indicate the centrality of writing and reconstruction to the story, and shall return to the question of psychology after having examined that of reading.

First, *writing*. It isn't just that Jessop is a novelist, living the kind of pre-war literary life that Ford himself led: speaking to literary clubs;

frequenting a night club based on the Cave of the Golden Calf, for which Ford (like Jessop) wrote a shadow-play (*RY* 430). Even though George Heimann is not a writer, the novel nonetheless associates him with writing.

It opens with Jessop's first sight of him, in a publisher's office which is at once tomb and womb, 'walled-in completely with books', 'A place where the Unborn float pallidly in dimnesses' (*MC* 1). George is there because the crooked publisher Mr. Podd hasn't honoured his agreement with George's sister to publish a translation by one of the novel's other writers, 'Professor Edouard Curtius, a preposterously important German poet' (*MC* 5). The book ends (bar the short coda of less than a page) with the tribulations of the pathologically inaccurate journalist, Plowright.

George's qualities are ones Ford particularly associated with writing. He comes to represent a union of romantic impulse and Olympian detachment – the sort of combination Ford particularly admired in Flaubert. When he conducts his own defence in court against the crooked publisher, Mr. Podd, Jessop says:

> And what really astonished me was that George could make that point so completely and so dispassionately. For, to tell the truth, I had always taken him as being so romantic and impulsive that I could never have expected him to be either collected or dispassionate. There he stood, however, drawing out my story in corroboration of his speech, which I had not heard, and getting it exactly to a hair. (*MC* 285)

It's a recurrent Fordian problem – how to combine sympathetic identification with 'the critical attitude'.[8] What is also telling here is how what's being described is the construction of a *story* – or rather, the *re*construction of a story – out of a sympathetic collaboration between speaker and listener, that could stand for the relationship between writer and reader.

This is our second concern. Ford often foregrounds the way retrospective narration is inevitably a *reconstructive* act. *The Marsden*

Case reaches back over the debris of the war to try to reconstruct the characters' pasts in the lost era of peace. Like *No Enemy: A Tale of Reconstruction*, it shows the survivors attempting to reconstruct the past, thus to redeem and to redress it. In this case – taking George's examination of Jessop in the witness-box as a figure for the act of piecing together a story – the allegory is more oblique. Though it should be noted that Jessop mentions the word 'story'; and that several of his other terms – of completeness, dispassionateness, romance, and exactitude – are ones Ford habitually uses in his literary criticism.

Our third, and chief concern here – with *reading* – needs to be seen as part of a broader Fordian attention to a whole range of modes of communication (and not-quite-communication). In *The Marsden Case* we find telephone calls; protracted correspondence; translation; psychological analysis; narration. More specifically, the novel is preoccupied with different forms of text: Jessop's novels and shadow play; Podd's doomed books; other novels and memoirs; Curtius' portentous poem; Plowright's journalism; letters; official forms; posters; legal documents. We generally see not just the texts, but – and this is crucial to my argument – someone *reading* them.

In the case of the late Earl's correspondence, we have: first a letter to George, of which Jessop says 'I could not read that letter: not consecutively. My mind would not stick to the longer sentences' (*MC* 154); then the correspondence between the Earl and Lady Ada, which Lady Ada has annotated and sent on to Jessop's mother, from amongst whose 'papers' Jessop discovers them, saying that he has 'only very lately had the time to look through' them (*MC* 172). In this case, then, we have five levels of reading: Lady Ada's original reading, being recalled as she re-reads the documents later and annotates them; Jessop reading them; his awareness that his mother has already read them; and finally the book's reader reading them. In another example, we see Jessop reading and re-reading a letter from George:

> I found that letter the other day, mildewed in the pillow flap of my valise, and when I re-read it I remembered powerfully that, when those words first came

to my eyes, I was standing in a corrugated iron hut, in the perpetual twilight of the North-east coast, with the wind blowing so through the walls that the illustrated papers, all damp as they were, were flying from the bamboo card tables on to the cokernut [*sic*] matting floors. And I remember thinking, with a sudden mental flash, that at one time I should not have been astonished if George himself had committed suicide.[9]

Here the Conradian decaying texts (mildewed letters, damp papers) cast Jessop as a writer – the biographer reconstructing a crumbling civilization – as well as a reader. The passage is a fine example of Ford's impressionism. The memory of how 'those words first came to my eyes' – the deixis is pronounced: '*those* words', *that* letter' – leads, with its slightly curious locution, to how the visual scene came back to his memory. The expression collapses the mnemonic into the readerly into the autobiographical. Then the sliding of tense, from 'I remembered' to 'I remember' takes Jessop, and the reader, back to that scene of re-reading. The tense slide has the effect of immediacy, drawing the reader into the experience; and simultaneously, this example conveys how powerfully the memory still affects Jessop: he just has to re-read the letter to remember the first reading, to be taken back to his earlier experiences. This intensity of attention given to the experience of reading can be found throughout Ford's work: especially in the novels, criticism, and reminiscences.

The Marsden Case abounds with such images of internal division, wandering attention. Some examples, though not explicitly *about* reading, are so suggestive of that experience, that they can be taken as figures *for* it. While Jessop waits outside a Whitehall office, where 'the floors were [. . .] littered with bits of soiled paper [. . .]', he demonstrates a wonderful Fordian attention to the way we inattend to our subliminal quirks: 'There I waited [. . . .] and I played a dismal game, stepping from piece to piece of paper in the attempt to work out some anodyne pattern' (*MC* 167). This detail too brings together many of the book's main themes. Jessop tries, at least with his 'subliminal self', to figure a carpet out of these degenerated former texts. It is a 'dismal game' (like the war, which was too often compared to one) not just because of the bureaucratic squalor, but because the protracted reconstruction in the novel – the attempt to work out George's family history exactly by stepping from one piece of paper to another, whether legal documents, will, memos – looks at this early stage in the book as if it is predestined to end dismally. An 'anodyne pattern' would be the subconscious soothing of a form of order perceived amidst official complexities; but it is also an outcome of the legal investigation that will end George's pain; as well as an inflexion which betrays the post-war need to get over the pain of battle and loss. Finally, the stepping from piece to piece is redolent of Ford's 'time-shift' method of juxtaposing disparate occasions into a significant pattern. In which case, the quest for an anodyne pattern could be a figure for writing too, as Ford the novel-designer wonders how the intricate anguish of this plot can possibly be resolved into the 'anodyne pattern' that is consolatory Romance.

It is also characteristic of Ford that episodes offer themselves as also in some way concerned with questions of writing and reading.[10] This incident is an example of how Ford's figures for reading or writing are frequently themselves instances of what they describe. The paper-stepping image is about wandering, divided minds; but its very suggestiveness divides the reader's mind, producing an awareness (even if subliminal) of other aspects. Fordian self-reflexiveness is not, in the terms of optics, total internal reflexion. He is no post-modernist. But we do often glimpse the art-object reflected in its subject; the scenes of the story transfigured by the reflected writer and reader.

The Marsden Case's concern with writing and reading is even more pervasive. There are two passages, one from each half of the novel, which are often discussed: the shadow play episode in the underground London night club; and the passage about the putative 'invisible tent' that the soldier vainly hopes will insulate him from domestic anxieties (*MC* 92-3; 127-8; 305). However, the connection between them has not been noticed. It is not just that both describe blank canvas surfaces (the sheet on which the shadows are cast; the tent), nor that both are predominantly visual images. Both can also be read as figures for the phenomenology of reading. We look at black signs on a white sheet, and imagine a reality beyond it.

Jessop calls his shadow play 'a burlesque of Romance', and the paraphrase he gives reveals it to be a proleptic burlesque of *The Marsden Case: A Romance*:

> A man is attacked by a cobra and an assassin at the same moment. The cobra bites his little finger – which of course is irrevocable death; but at the pain he starts aside, and the descending yataghan of the assassin cuts off his little finger. So the hero is saved from his oriental adventures – the assassin was, of course, a Deceived Husband – and returns to Europe with a heroine from behind the grille of a harem, to open a tobacco shop. (*MC* 127-8)[11]

The cobra and assassin could stand for Miss Jeaffreson and Mr. Podd. (Biographically, both burlesque and novel might express a feeling that the war had enabled Ford to uncoil himself from Violet Hunt, and set up house with Stella Bowen.) Clarice Honeywill declaims 'This not very amusing story' with 'an awful voice in which every word was clearer than type'. This transcendence of the written – or, rather, the printed ('clearer than type') – coincides with Clarice's physical transcendence of the sheet:

> And then, suddenly . . . I had not the least idea how she did it: the light did not even go out. She must have had a superb athletic physique; for there she was, crosslegged, in the middle of the stage, in front of the sheet [. . .] (*MC* 128)

Reading the shadow play of writing can transform the shadowy absent into the colourful, sensuous present ('in scarlet trousers, rolling a cigarette'; *MC* 128). Voice can be clearer than type, and conjure the shadow into substance. This is the (logocentric) magic of Romance: the 'power of reading'. ('In the beginning the power to write – and still more the power of reading! – ranked with the Black Arts'.)[12] The passage about the invisible tent considers magic too:

I used to think that, once out there, we should be surrounded by a magic and invisible tent that would keep from us all temporal cares. But we are not so surrounded, and it is not like that [. . . .] round your transparent tent, the old evils, the old heartbreaks and the old cruelties are unceasingly at work. (*MC* 305)

'I *used* to think that [. . .] we *should* be surrounded [. . . .] But we *are* not so surrounded'. The sliding tense here moves from the war – then and there – back to the present. It is far from careless. Part of the point of that present is again the Impressionist dictum of immediacy: it takes us back to Jessop's remembered experience in France. But it also hints at how the longing for a release from all our temporal cares is itself temporal, present, and cannot be banished to the past, or to somewhere quite other. The element of escapism in Fordian Romance is part of its rendering of the human desire for escape, and need of Romance.

Jessop's metaphor is a tantalizingly impossible one. How can an *invisible* tent screen anything? The impossibility is recognized in the shift from 'invisible' to 'transparent': as with the window in the essay 'On Impressionism', there is a glint of the medium itself: 'glass so bright that whilst you perceive through it a landscape or a backyard, you are aware that, on its surface, it reflects a face of a person behind you'. Near the beginning, Jessop connects the idea of a transparent medium and the telling of stories, in a passage which casts him as the characteristic Fordian *homo duplex*:[13]

> In short, I had a life of my own, and my thoughts were already well occupied. So that a good many of the adventures of my young friend Heimann passed as if behind a transparent veil, and, if I don't tell them straightforwardly, as stories are usually told, that is simply because I had so many things on my mind. (*MC* 18.)

The book is thus presented as, itself, a shadow play, played out on the page-like transparent veil of Jessop's preoccupied, enervated consciousness. *The Marsden Case* is pervaded by shadows, whether visual, tonal, or psychological. George's foredoomed (attempted) suicide is predictably set in *chiaroscuro*: he is rescued by Plowright and a policeman, who 'lowered George into the car amidst the beechen shadows' (*MC* 320). It is only the shadow of a death, but, as suggested, it stands for the war's actual dead, whom Ford often visualized as an ominous shadow. 'You would have thought those people would have shown some decency with the shadow of death falling right across the land. But they didn't.'[14]

This last image perhaps best captures the relationship of *The Marsden Case* to the war. It is not a war novel because it doesn't render trench experience. But the shadow of the war falls across its pages. In particular, it falls between the pre-war and post-war parts of its diptych structure. The diptych form is thus more than a simple juxtaposition. It is a large-scale structural counterpart to the registered self-suppression of Ford's characters and his style. We are conscious of what is suppressed, and also of the act of suppression, the dignity of which guarantees the authenticity of the suffering being suppressed. In both *Some Do Not . . .* and *The Marsden Case*, the transition from the pre-war to the wartime to the post-war draws attention to the elided war-experience. The war is the absent subject for which the book is (like most of Ford's best work) an elegy. The pressing absence between the two parts becomes an abyss. A powerful passage from *It Was the Nightingale* describes how the ordeal of the war corresponded to dropping into abysses:

> You may say that everyone who had taken physical part in the war was then mad. No one could have come through that shattering experience and still view life and mankind with any normal vision. In those days you saw objects that the earlier mind labelled as *houses*. They had been used to seem cubic and solid permanences. But we had seen Ploegsteert where it had been revealed that men's dwellings were thin shells that could be crushed as walnuts are crushed [. . . .] Nay, it had been revealed to you that beneath Ordered Life itself was stretched, the merest film with, beneath it, the abysses of Chaos. One had come from the frail shelters of the Line to a world that was more frail than any canvas hut. (*IWN* 48-9)

This is a re-imagining of the 'invisible tent' idea, as the images of the 'film' and the 'canvas hut' make plain. Though here it is more successful, its precariousness more vivid and disturbing. Part of that precariousness is created by the way the phrase 'Ordered Life' hesitates between referring to the material realities of civilization (houses, walnuts) or to the semi-transparent pages through which literature renders civilization. Books too are 'Ordered Life'.[15]

One way of reading these figures of the invisible tent or transparent veil is of a projection (it is almost a cinematic image; that of the shadow play performed behind a white sheet, though different, equally connotes the cinematic screen); a projection of the self away from the Front. This is certainly the force of Ford's reminiscences of reading while he was on the Western Front. In these, the readings take him out of present space and time, and superimpose alternative realities upon the war.[16] Paul Fussell has written of how strikingly the First World War was a 'literary war'; how much reading was done during it.[17] Ford's imagining of reading in the context of war suggests that the reason may be to do with more than trying to fill in the time: it was also because reading ministers to fantasies of escape, or the wish that the power of writing might magically protect, render the subject as omnipotent and invulnerable as any romance hero.

II

The discussion of writing and reading has necessarily shaded off into a discussion of the fourth concern: *psychology* – because Ford's Impressionism is primarily concerned with the psychological effects of art (and, as in the passage about Ordered Life, with the relation between art's effects and other kinds of psychological effect). *The Marsden Case* is preoccupied with similar attentions to the psychological effects of war. Like *A Call* – one of the first novels, if not the first, to feature a psychological specialist – it is not so much a psychological novel as a novel about psychology. Having suffered under several barbaric regimes of German 'nerve cures' after his 1904 breakdown, Ford had his own reasons for being ambivalent about psychology. He appears to have consulted a nerve specialist after being shell-shocked at the battle of the Somme, and to have felt that the doctor – who was probably Henry Head, one of the leading English neurologists of the day – had betrayed his confidences.[18] (Perhaps he also felt threatened by a rival narrative mode.) *The Marsden Case* bristles with such ambivalence. Clarice's father, Dr Robins, is accused of having 'put into [George's] head ideas of nervous symptoms that would have been just as well not there. He was a specialist; but a specialist up to that time repressed' (*MC* 257). Behind the facile joke about psychological expertise as itself a mental disorder, there is an alarming psychological truth: mental illness *can* be produced by putting 'ideas' into someone's head. Delusions *are* ideas; complexes could be described as unconscious ideas; nervous symptoms do get produced by repressed ideas. In *The Good Soldier* Ford showed how Ashburnham's kissing of the nurse-maid in the train 'had put ideas into his head' – ideas of passion that drive him to despair and suicide (*GS* 184).[19] When he declares his love for his ward, Nancy Rufford, 'It was as if his passion for her hadn't existed; as if the very words that he spoke, without knowing that he spoke them, created his passion as they went along' (*GS* 137). Characteristically, Ford is not only interested in his characters' psychology, but also in that of his readers. The writer's words create the characters and their passions for the reader. Ford knows that his job as author is to put ideas into his reader's head. And that it carries with it dangers and responsibilities. The ideas an author puts in can drive certain (or perhaps, *un*certain?) readers off their heads. As Nancy, for example, begins to lose her mental balance when she reads about the Brand divorce case in the newspaper, and becomes haunted by the new awareness of the possibilities of adultery and divorce.

The other nerve specialist in *The Marsden Case* is shown as ineptly summoning up the very shadows he should be exorcizing; but again in a way that alludes to the reading experience. As with our recursive reading of Dowell's recursive telling, so when Clarice takes George to this 'soul-straightener' to relieve his anxiety, the treatment consists in re-living the disturbing past that induced the anxiety: 'that fellow made the whole of his past life rush before him in a few seconds [. . .]' (*MC* 316). This – characteristically of *The Marsden Case* – seeks the pathos of a specious inevitability, suggesting that it is the rapid reviewing of a life in the moments before death (as, conventionally, before drowning). But it also suggests the way a novel's *progression d'effet* strives to convey, by foreshortening, the effect of a life's progression: *The Marsden Case* makes George's life flash before us in a few hours.

Arthur Mizener objected that the characters are 'more eccentric than Ford recognizes'.[20] Yet not only are Jessop and George recognizably (and recognized as) neurasthenic; the claim is also made that their eccentricity is more representative than it might seem: 'There are more of those in the country than you would think' (*MC* 162). Like Freud, Ford reveals how widespread is the 'psychopathology of everyday life', and how self-serving and self-deceiving are society's attempts to fence out madness. (Compare: 'everyone who had taken physical part in the war was then mad'.) Ford still worried about the question of representativeness, however. After he had finished *Parade's End* he voiced a doubt about Tietjens' eccentricity:

> the defect of all novel-writing is that, as a rule, the novelist – Heaven help him – must needs select unusual, hypersensitized souls to endure the vicissitudes that he is pleased to make them endure, and that makes him lose half the game with the normal reader. I remember very well [. . .] thinking to myself when about half-way through a novel about the late war, 'Well, my central character is altogether such a queer, unusual fellow that I do not see how anyone is going much to sympathise with him in his misfortunes.[21]

As Ford recognizes here, it isn't only in *The Marsden Case* that 'hypersensitized souls' are foregrounded. They appear, doubled or proliferating, throughout his oeuvre: Grimshaw *and* Leicester in *A Call*; Dowell, Leonora, *and* Nancy Rufford; George *and* Jessop; not only Tietjens, but *also* Sylvia, McKechnie, and 'Breakfast' Duchemin; Henry *and* Hugh in *The Rash Act* and its sequel.

It is the hyper-sensitized reader who will approximate to the Fordian ideal of 'vicarious experience'. Ford uses the experiences of the person reading as a figure for the predicament of modern humanity in general. The doubleness of our response to his hyper-sensitized characters (a combination of sympathetic identification and the ironic detachment of the critical attitude) mirrors the sensibility of a nerve-seared generation. Yet Ford's homologies between author, characters, and reader can have alarming implications given the mental states of many of his characters. As Dr Johnson feared, vicarious experience is itself a delusion. Dowell's words about needing to fend off maddening realities – 'these delusions are necessary to keep us going [. . .]' (*GS* 57) – are unnervingly applicable to writers and readers of fiction, who need delusions to keep them going.[22]

To investigate these implications we need to consider other examples of mental division, and their relation to ideas of the will. Ford, as so often, is close to the Freudian idea of the unconscious, though he prefers his own terminology of the 'subconscious self', 'subliminal self', or 'underself' as opposed to the 'surface self' or 'conscious mind'.[23] Ford's terms imply some indefinite and intermittent, yet nevertheless pressing, awareness of these marginal mental activities: activities which the conscious self has often suppressed.

The 'subliminal' or subconscious (rather than unconscious) awareness of mind is related to those subtle effects of prose which we often register in just such a subliminal way; a half-consciousness of the medium through which we are imagining. The ability of the written word (indeed, *any* artistic medium) to mobilize our subliminal sense enables an artist like Ford to produce in the mind of the reader effects enough like the volitional crises of his characters to amplify our sympathy. His prose is alert to the way human relations can be fraught with struggles of will; and to the way reading involves a degree of willing surrender to the volition of the author.

The Marsden Case contrasts Clarice Honey*will*, George's good angel who 'could get her own way against the wills of legions of men' (*MC* 292), with Miss Jeaffreson, the exponent of a willful materialism, who is writing a volume as appalling as it is unnecessary: a *Child's*

147

Guide to Nietzsche. When she is alone with Mr. Heimann (alias Earl Marsden):

> 'with all the force of her nature,' she began to will him to speak to her. He was holding a solid book, of the memoir type, on high, rather close to his eyes; his face was hidden. She went on 'willing.' (*MC* 52)

'[S]olid' is a magnificent Fordian *mot juste*. It captures the way the reading public (to Ford's perpetual chagrin) considers memoir-type books as 'sounder' than novels; it plays on how Ford's reader is *at this moment* (like you) holding a book; but it also acknowledges the lack of solidity of what we read – the way what Henry James called 'solidity of specification' must strive against the inherent immateriality of the form, the dissolution of its accumulating 'matter'.[24] Miss Jeaffreson appears as an anti-novelist here, coercing her silent non-listener to attend to her personality. The inverted commas in the quotation remind us that Jessop's *style indirect libre* is based, for this portion of the narrative, on Miss Jeaffreson's version: ostensibly they are her own words. Highlighting them like this alerts us to the very forcefulness of her willpower. She is even able (like a manipulative novelist) to stop people speaking: 'How she suppressed the Professor without herself speaking I do not know. It was magic of the will' (*MC* 73).

In her case too, it is not simply a matter of *conscious* willing:

> It was at this point that Miss Jeaffreson suddenly asked Mr. Heimann if he had made his will. She said that the words sounded like a thunderclap.
> I can imagine that they upset her a great deal. Nothing could have been further from her conscious mind than to ask such a question. She said that it was one of the most extraordinary instances of action by a subliminal self that her experience had afforded her [. . . .] I am inclined to think that all through this interview [. . .] at the bottom of her mind there had always been the passionate desire to know whether Mr. Heimann had made his will! (*MC* 56-7)

It is characteristic of the way this book refracts the war that Ford imagines the verbal equivalent of something like shell-shock: 'the words sounded like a thunderclap'. (Compare Jessop's reaction when he hears Mr. Podd shouting at George: 'You bl---y bastard!': 'I think those words detonated more than any sound I have ever heard'; *MC* 12.) In this particular explosion of the subconscious, note how Miss Jeaffreson's crisis of conscious will, soon after she has 'willed' Heimann to speak, elicits her question about his testamentary 'will'.

Ford's unease with willful women is matched by his anxiety about male will-lessness. The 'most ghastly feeling' George ever has in his life is 'the dread that he might act in spite of his will; or even unconsciously' (*MC* 217). As Mizener argued, this probably became one of Ford's greatest dreads during and after the war.[25] Jessop shares this feeling of mental disintegration. Before the war he attributes it to conflicts of passion, but it offers another example of Ford's superimposing of pre-war and post-war, war and passion, since it anticipates Jessop's post-war nervous debility:

> Besides, I had just lately [. . .] been so badly manhandled by a woman that half the time, even then, I did not rightly know what I was doing. I would see things vividly for an hour or so, and then . . . dimness – a wavering in which I could hear myself speaking collectedly or with cynicism. That is the worst sort of 'underself' to have! (*MC* 84)

This could be taken as an oblique comment on how writing can mobilise the 'underself'. Seeing things vividly for an hour or so would correspond to the writer's visionary experience which then needs to be translated into words; to become the reader's vicarious vision. But then as the writer emerges from the vision he catches himself talking – suddenly becomes aware of the activity of his voice, of his composing, collecting mind. That sense of a split between the self that's talking and the self that's hearing could be disconcerting enough (like the moment of waking in which you think you have been talking in a dream). For the writer the fear here would be that the writing was expressing something beyond the control of the conscious mind. Ford's emphasis on technical self-consciousness suggests that it mattered deeply to him to be in control of his art; he reserved sarcasm for the notion that an aspiring author need only 'put some vine-leaves in his hair and write' (*AL* 293).

The other point to be made about Jessop's account of his 'underself' is that it also evokes reading. The experience of reading Ford's impressionist prose combines (or alternates between) seeing things vividly and hearing the collected speaking voice of the narrative, voiced by one's own imagined voice in the mind's ear. In this case the dimness and wavering would correspond to the way really engrossed reading can make you oblivious to your surroundings, your body. Reading can create the impression of an 'underself' by creating the effect of other consciousnesses within the arena of the reader's consciousness. Georges Poulet has written of the reading-act: 'because of the strange invasion of my person by the thoughts of another, I am a self who is granted the experience of thinking thoughts foreign to him. I am the subject of thoughts other than my own'.[26]

Ford's great precursor in attending to this relation between reading and the will is Marcel Proust, whom he considered translating after the war, and whom he records as influencing the conception of *Parade's End*.[27] Proust too had suffered from mental illness. George Painter describes how: 'During the first half of 1905 he had conscientiously read up the works of French specialists in nervous ailments [. . . .] the very title of Dr. Ribot's *Diseases of the Will* was a reproach which struck home [. . .]'. In 'Sur la lecture', the preface to his translation of Ruskin's *Sesame and Lilies*, Proust objects to the 'preponderant role in life' that Ruskin assigns to reading. His wonder at 'that fruitful miracle of a communication in the midst of solitude' is offset by his sense of its limitations: 'Reading is at the threshold of spiritual life; it can introduce us to it; it does not constitute it'. Proust's terms here are close to Ford's: silent communication in solitude; reading as the energizer of intellectual power in solitude which conversation tends to dissipate; reading as an activity, as travel; reading as an illusion of escape.[28]

Proust's grasp of the volitional ambiguities of the reading act, and its rewards, enables him to make explicit the kind of understanding that is implicit in works like *The Good Soldier* and *Parade's End*. The following is some of the best criticism of those recursive books, even though written before them:

> We feel quite truly that our wisdom begins where that of the author ends, and we would like to have him give us answers, while all he can do is give us desires. And these desires he can arouse in us only by making us contemplate the supreme beauty which the last effort of his art has permitted him to reach. But by a singular and, moreover, providential law of mental optics (a law which perhaps signifies that we can receive the truth from nobody, and that we must create it ourselves), that which is the end of their wisdom appears to us as but the beginning of ours, so that it is at the moment when they have told us all they could tell us, that they create in us the feeling that they have told us nothing yet. (*On Reading*, pp. 35-7)

This, we might say, is why *A la recherche* must end with the decision to write *A la recherche*. It also supplies the necessary qualification to Poulet's argument. Reading is a creative collaboration between the consciousnesses of writer and reader, rather than the disappearance of the reader's consciousness within the writer's. Writing is a conscious art; reading is only a partial surrender of one's reading-consciousness to the author. The history of Modernism removes Proust's tentative brackets, to show us authors discarding received truths in favour of truths they have created by (and for) themselves; discarding weak-willed, passive, consumptive reading in favour of an active production of the work. In the years of post-war reconstruction, the emphasis is not (as it would be later) on deconstruction and 'the death of the author', but on the reconstruction of literature. As with the mythic, allusive methods of Joyce and Eliot (though less scholastically), writing and reading for Ford are acts of reconstruction.

The argument so far has tried to bring out the book's subtle exploration of topics Ford knew well – the war, psychology, reconstruction – by showing how he characteristically negotiates them obliquely, through experiences he knew even better – writing and reading.[29] It is part of a larger argument, rehearsed elsewhere, that at the centre of Ford's contribution – to fiction, to autobiography, to criticism – is his unique and sustained re-imagining of the experiences of reading and writing; and that his technically self-conscious imagination often finds in his craft itself his best metaphors for the states of mind he describes.[30] When Ford said: 'I believe that, as "treatment", it's the best thing I've done [. . .]', this may have been not just because he felt the thematic material had been particularly well-handled, say, or that he had found more *mots justes* than usual; but because 'treatment' was itself foregrounded to a greater extent than in his previous work (even than in *The Good Soldier*, where Dowell is only *like* a novelist; someone naïvely wondering about how to compose, rather than consciously rendering.[31] Like most of his work, *The Marsden Case* can be read (in the kind of oblique ways I have been illustrating) as an allegory of literary 'treatment'. It works through some of Ford's deepest thoughts about what literary treatment is: how (in Gertrude Stein's wonderfully illuminative tautology) writing is written; how, as we might re-write it, how reading is read.[32]

Read thus, the literariness of the plot might seem more defensible. Furthermore, 'treatment' can of course be taken in another sense. Psychological treatment. The pun is an essential one, since *The Marsden Case*, like *Parade's End* after it, is massively concerned not just with the damage caused by the war to minds as well as bodies, but also with its treatment. Jessop describes himself as having 'the insatiable craving of one nearly come back into active life – for the details of active life' (*MC* 326). 'I was supposed to be cured', he tells us (*MC* 324). And if we hear a lingering disturbance in his 'insatiable craving', the sentence makes us wonder how far our readerly craving for 'the details of active life' is separable from pathological desire.

What this suggests is the possibility of literary treatment *as* therapeutic treatment. The possibility that the reconstruction of narrative is a vital element of the reconstruction of traumatised psyches. After all, the notion of 'reconstruction' underwent a change in Ford's consciousness as a result of the war. In *The Good Soldier*, the past has to be reconstructed, but the reconstructed past, and the effort of its reconstruction, proves devastating and draining. After the war, reconstruction becomes imperative and redemptive: somehow the mad reconstruction of his father's death saves George from repeating it. This may reflect a feeling of Ford's that his near-death experience of the war had allowed him to be reborn. And that writing about that experience, in his earliest attempts such as 'True Love & a G. C. M.', or 'Mr. Croyd', had helped him get 'over the nerve tangle of the war and feel able at last really to write again [. . .]'.[33]

The literature of death can produce a comparable effect on its readers too. Perhaps one reason why reading of such things as war, death, tragedy, is more consoling than it should be is that we have the experience of vicariously dying, but surviving. In other words, that, phantasmatically, at least, we emerge from an engrossing book reborn: transformed. Milan Kundera says that his fictional characters cross boundaries he has not.[34] Reading of death, near-death, suicide, near-suicide, could be seen as functioning in similarly vicarious ways: as taking us over boundaries we have not crossed, or not yet.

In the light of the twentieth-century's long psycho-analytic turn, it may seem a truism to equate art and therapy: as D. H. Lawrence does, for example, saying: 'One sheds one's sicknesses in books – repeats and presents again one's emotions to be master of them'.[35] Yet Ford's own experience of both nervous breakdown and cure, both before and after the war, makes him part of modern literature's increasing engagement with psycho-analytic modes. And in practice, the writing of *The Marsden Case* was indeed effective treatment for Ford as an author, enabling him to go on to write one of his greatest masterpieces, *Parade's End*.

NOTES

1. Pound, '[The Inquest]' [1924?], *Pound/Ford*, ed. Brita Lindberg-Seyersted, London: Faber and Faber, 1983, p.70. For a fuller discussion of *Mr. Fleight* (London: Howard Latimer, 1913), see Saunders, *Ford Madox Ford: A Dual Life*, Oxford: Oxford University Press: 1996, vol. I, pp.378-80.

2. Ford to Pound, 26 July 1920: *PF* 33; and 29 July 1920: *LF* 118-9. Ludwig wrongly annotates this – and other letters on pp.114 and 130 – as referring to *MC*; whereas 'Mr Croyd' is much more probable. See Saunders, vol. II, 571 n.3.

3. See the excerpts published in Ford's *War Prose*, ed. Max Saunders, Manchester: Carcanet, 1999, pp.265-71.

4. Robert Green, *Ford Madox Ford: Prose and Politics*, Cambridge: Cambridge University Press, 1981, p.127. Paul Wiley attributes George's suicide-attempt to his fear of publicity: *Novelist of Three Worlds: Ford Madox Ford*, Syracuse, N.Y.: Syracuse University Press, 1962, p.209; but this kind of public event inside the world of the novel is not what Green has in mind; he means fiction should reflect externally verifiable historical realities. For other good criticism of *MC*, see Ann Barr Snitow, *Ford Madox Ford and the Voice of Uncertainty*, Baton Rouge and London: Louisiana State University Press, 1984.

5. Mizener, *The Saddest Story*, London: The Bodley Head, 1972, p.370. He also observes that *SDN* presents 'an England that Englishmen generally will have some difficulty in recognizing' (p.257).

6. See Saunders, vol. II, 110-16. For example, Jessop recalls being preoccupied by 'the deadness in the voice of George Heimann' during the trial scene: a phrase which perhaps suggests (misleadingly) that George is himself about to die, or that his voice somehow stands for the war's deaths (*MC* 284).

7. Saunders, vol. II, 110-16. What follows in the present essay is a revised version of pp.98-114 of Chapter 3 of my Doctoral dissertation, 'Ford Madox Ford and the Reading of Prose', University of Cambridge, 1985.

8. Saunders, vol. II, 400-01.

9. *The Marsden Case*, London: Duckworth, 1923, p.202. Jessop has just read the postscript in which George, with Dowellian anti-climax, said he 'supposed' Jessop 'knew that his poor father had committed suicide'.

10. *Ladies Whose Bright Eyes,* for example, is also susceptible of being read in terms of the experience of reading. See Saunders, 'To Make You See: La Metafisica della letteratura in Ford Madox Ford', in *Scrittura e Sperimentazione in Ford Madox Ford,* ed. Vita Fortunati and Rafaella Baccolini, Florence: Alinea Editrice, 1994, pp.59-89. Also the later 'double' novels. See Saunders, 'Duality, Reading and Art in Ford's Last Novels', *Contemporary Literature,* 30:2 (Summer 1989), 299-320.

11. Ford returned to this story in 'The Khitmutgar of Ootacamund', *Your Life,* 3:2 (Aug. 1938), 96-8. The 8 pp. typescript is at Cornell University Library, headed 'The Narrowest Escape from Death', together with an untitled 3 pp. version. A letter to George Bye shows that another provisional title for this story was 'Near Death' (1 April 1938: Cornell). The opening words are 'This is the story of the narrowest escape from death ever experienced by mortal man'.

12. 'Stocktaking: Towards a Re-Valuation of English Literature, by Daniel Chaucer. V.', *transatlantic review,* 1:5 (May 1924), 321-29 (p. 321).

13. 'On Impressionism', *Poetry and Drama,* 2 (June and December 1914), 167-75, 323-34 (p. 174). See Max Saunders, 'Duality, Reading, and Art in Ford's Last Novels'.

14. See for example 'A Day of Battle', *The Ford Madox Ford Reader,* ed. Sondra Stang, Manchester: Carcanet, 1986, pp.456-61 (p.461); and *NMP* 140. *MC* 197.

15. See also my discussion of this passage in 'A Life in Writing: Ford Madox Ford's Dispersed Autobiographies', *Antæus,* no. 56 (Spring 1986), 47-69 (p. 56).

16. See *War Prose,* pp.230-5.

17. Paul Fussell, *The Great War and Modern Memory,* New York and London: Oxford University Press, 1975, Chapter 5. See also Imogen Gassert, 'In a Foreign Field: What Soldiers in the Trenches Liked to Read', *TLS,* 10 May 2002, 17-19.

18. See for example *RY* 266-9; and Mizener 91-100. Robert and Marie Secor, in *The Return of the Good Soldier: Ford Madox Ford and Violet Hunt's 1917 Diary* ELS monograph series, no. 30, Victoria, B.C., 1983, p.68n, note that Ford was threatening to prosecute 'Dr Head' in July 1917. The presence of a letter from Henry Head to Violet Hunt (7 November 1922) in Cornell University Library's collection of Ford and Hunt papers makes the identification probable. Virginia Woolf was taken to see Head, who is thought to be an original for Sir William Bradshaw in *Mrs Dalloway.* Roger Poole, *The Unknown Virginia Woolf,* Cambridge:Cambridge University Press, 1978, pp.137-47. See Saunders, vol. II, 38.

19. Citations from *The Good Soldier* are taken from the World's Classics edition, ed. Thomas C. Moser, Oxford: Oxford University Press, 1990.

20. Mizener 494.

21. 'A Note by way of a Preface' to Peregrine Acland's *All Else is Folly* (London: Constable, 1929), pp.vii-xi (pp.vii-viii). Excerpted in *War Prose*, pp.193-5.

22. Ford's engagements with the notion of 'vicarious experience' are discussed in my 'Ford Madox Ford and the Reading of Prose', pp.40-8. Also see Saunders, vol. II, 400.

23. See *MC* 20, 57, 56, 20, 56 respectively. Also see *NE* 37, 80, and *RY* 302 for 'subconscious mind'; *NMP* 267, for 'subordinate minds' (there applied to General Campion's militarist mental hierarchy); and *SDN* 229, for 'under mind'.

24. James, 'The Art of Fiction', *Longman's Magazine*, 4 (September 1884), 502-21 (p.510).

25. Mizener, pp.288-9, 603 n.37. His view is borne out by the passages from 'Mr. Croyd' printed in the *War Prose*.

26. Poulet, 'Phenomenology of Reading', *New Literary History*, 1:1 (October 1969), 53-68 (p.56).

27. Ford to Ezra Pound, 30 August 1920: *LF* 122. *IWN* 194-5.

28. Painter, *Marcel Proust*, 2 vols, London: Chatto & Windus, 1959-65, II, p.52. Proust, *On Reading*, trans. Jean Autret and William Burford, London: Souvenir Press, 1972, pp.27, 31, 39, 55, 31, 45, 61. For a further discussion of Ford's ideas about literature and solitude, see Saunders, 'Ford Madox Ford and the Reading of Prose', pp.22-33.

29. In 'A Day of Battle', for example, his immediate reaction to his trench experience is articulated in terms of why he finds it impossible to describe it. *War Prose*, pp.36-42.

30. See Saunders, 'Ford Madox Ford and the Reading of Prose'.

31. *LF* 149; compare p.138, where Ford says much the same to Jepson. For critics praising the literary treatment, in addition to the reviews listed in D. D. Harvey, *Ford Madox Ford: 1873-1939: A Bibliography of Works and Criticism*, Princeton: Princeton University Press, 1962, pp. 339-40, see Mizener 491, 494; Robert Green, p.126; and Snitow 202.

32. Gertrude Stein, *How Writing is Written*, ed. Robert Bartlett Haas, Los Angeles:

THE MARSDEN CASE

Black Sparrow Press, 1974.

33. 'True Love & a G. C. M.' was first published in *War Prose*, pp.77-139. Ford to H. G. Wells, 14 Oct. 1923: *LF* 154.

34. Milan Kundera, *The Unbearable Lightness of Being,* translated by Michael Henry Heim, London: Faber and Faber, 1985, p.221.

35. D. H. Lawrence, quoted by Aldous Huxley, *The Letters of D. H. Lawrence*, London: Heinemann, 1932, p.ix.

BEYOND THE PLEASURE PRINCIPLE:

THE RASH ACT AND *HENRY FOR HUGH*

David Ayers

> My RASH ACT which is more like what I want to write than anything I have done for years came out on the 24th ult and has naturally been absolutely submerged.
>
> Letter to Ezra Pound, 8 March 1933 (*P/F* 120)

If a reading of Ford is to be anything other than an archaeology, Graham Greene's contention that 'no one in our century ... has been more attentive to the craft of letters'[1] must be brought squarely to face the least unknown of Ford's later novels, *The Rash Act* (1933).[2] For Alan Judd, one of Ford's strongest contemporary advocates, this novel 'is a flowering of ripeness and it should be read.'[3] However, many commentators on Ford have entirely ignored *The Rash Act* and its sequel, *Henry For Hugh* (1934).[4] This latter was described by Pound as 'irritatin' an meritorious – as usual,'[5] a judgement confirmed by Richard Cassell who classifies both novels as 'engaging literary oddities.'[6] Even to ignore these novels in a critical account of Ford is to acknowledge that there lies behind them a remarkable, though somewhat obscure and even skewed ambition on Ford's part. This analysis aims to discover something of the principles which organise this pair of novels.

I take it that, in part when we read Ford, we will do so in terms of the political aesthetics which is now so central to our understanding of modernism. Here, the agrarianism of Ford's work in the Thirties, which takes an idealised Provence and a mythified Great Trade Route as its central images, is recognisably related to the anti-industrialism of Eliot, Pound, Lewis and, of particular interest here, Allen Tate, whom Ford befriended in 1925 or 1927.[7] Though their politics differed, Ford attempted to woo Tate with his vision of Provence as an agricultural idyll of small producers (e.g. *GTR* 78-9, 86-7), and as 'a frame of mind to which, unless we return, our occidental civilisation is doomed' (*GTR* 39). Tate responded with his poem 'The Mediterranean'.[8] Ford in his turn dedicated *Provence* (1935) to Tate. In *Great Trade Route* (1937), which advanced a dualistic view of European civilisation as a conflict between Mediterranean civilisation and Nordic bloodthirstiness, Ford expressed his solidarity with the South by claiming that Europe was divided by 'a sort of Mason-Dixon line' (*GTR* 41). Provence provides the main location for *The Rash Act*, and Ford's theses about the good life are a central part of the conceptual structure. The central plot, which has a failed American transform himself into a successful Englishman, equally testifies to a grand cultural agenda – as well as to the violation of earlier strictures on allegory in *the transatlantic review*: 'the allegory may come into its own again,' Ford remarks ironically, 'The portents are not lacking!' (*CW* 27)

To judge by Ford's comments on his own novel in a short article for the London-based *Week-End Review* (*Reader* 266-8), *The Rash Act* was to have been the first of a number of volumes dealing with the fate of one Henry Martin Aluin Smith, an American businessman ruined by the Wall Street Crash.[9] In fact only one volume was to follow, which concludes the narrative in the form of what Ford called 'an inverted detective story' (*Reader* 269). This second volume was published only in the United States, even though sales of the first volume had been better in Britain,[10] yet it does not read as a hasty conclusion to a series. Rather, it is difficult to imagine how the almost fairy-tale plot could have been drawn out further, and questionable whether it should have been drawn out for so long.

Some of the main concerns of *The Rash Act* are outlined in the note for the *Week-End Review*:

> *The Rash Act* is the elaborately time-shifted story of a man driven to the very edge of suicide and almost over. The world-crisis has ruined him. The writer's main impulse was what may be called historic. He desired to tell that story in an atmosphere of our own world with the effects and echoes of the

Crisis and its machinery creeping in as nowadays it does for all of us. It would be too much to say that the writer also had the purpose of familiarizing Europe with the real America of quiet homes, old memories, entrenched traditions and cultivated, almost hypersensitized people – as opposed to the gangster, high-jacker, big business visage that America usually presents to these shores. *The Rash Act* might or might not serve that public purpose. At any rate, for the last twenty years the writer, always a wanderer, has had the idea of familiarizing widely separated peoples the one with the other somewhere at the back of his mind. (*Reader* 267)

The novel is, to say the least, 'elaborately time-shifted': it employs all the art and seeming artlessness of *The Good Soldier* and *Parade's End*, privileging the vagaries of memory, and valorising the anecdotal over the grand chronological narrative of a capitalised History.

Thematically, there is a consciously Jamesian concern to negotiate the gap between American and European culture. Ford announced proudly to Pound: 'You will find more in it about your country than all the belchings poor Bob [McAlmon] ever belched.'[11] In part, Ford aspires to place himself in the tradition of Sherwood Anderson and his documentation of small town America in *Winesburg, Ohio* (1919) – Ford's protagonist is from Springfield, Ohio. In part, he wishes to emulate the naturalism of Dreiser, acknowledging the debt by giving his protagonist a 'Sister Carrie' (whose history contrasts sharply with that of Dreiser's own *Sister Carrie* [1900]). Because he so unremittingly identified himself as an 'impressionist', it is perhaps insufficiently acknowledged that Ford's work is closely akin to naturalism in terms of its aspiration to document cause and effect: 'Before everything a story must convey a sense of inevitability' (*JC* 218-9). In *The Rash Act*, these ambitions are manifested in the complex potted histories given to each of the more important figures. These histories, small gems in themselves, suggest the complex, cross-cultural origins of the individual: the French New Yorker, the German American, the American German, the small town American who marries into European aristocracy and so on. These portraits are naturalistically particular, and advance Ford's anti-nationalistic, localist thought by modelling not only America but the whole of the West as a racial melting-pot.

The Rash Act deals with the crossing of the fates of an American and an Englishman who share the same surname and initials and have a notable physical resemblance. The American, Henry Martin Aluin Smith, is 'free, male and twenty-one. Rising thirty-six, that is to say' (*RA* 10). He has rejected a life in the family candy business – 'Pisto-Brittle' of Springfield, Ohio – in favour of a career as a writer. As a writer he has been a failure: his one published work, an anthology of gossip from antiquity to modern times called (a quiet irony) *Be Thou Chaste*, has appeared illustrated by an unscrupulous publisher with images of supposedly ancient, toga-clad orgiasts who resemble better-known members of the American expatriate colony in Paris to which Henry Martin belongs. The book has had a *succès de scandale*, earning the author entirely the wrong kind of literary reputation and nothing else, as his publisher will not pay him. Henry Martin's immediate problem is financial. He is cut off from his father's wealth by his rejection of the family business. What he did possess has come to him through his mother. Much of this has been drained from him by his now estranged wife, who has left him for a lesbian relationship with a Mrs Percival, whom Henry Martin had deludedly presumed to have an interest not in his wife but in himself. The wife, Alice, is now divorcing him at the point of his final ruin, which has been brought about by the Wall Street Crash and the general depression. An ill-advised investment has destroyed what little means he had and, rather than get a job, Henry Martin opts for suicide, as did numerous ruined speculators in the aftermath of 1929.

The night before the planned suicide Henry Martin meets his near namesake, Hugh Monckton Allardyce Smith. The two have a close physical resemblance and are unknowingly related, having a grand-father in common. Hugh Monckton also plans suicide, as he discloses to Henry Martin in drunken conversation, not for money but for love. Hugh Monckton is English, and is the heir of an immensely successful luxury car business which is so powerful that it has bucked the trend of the depression and continued to thrive. Monckton is projected as an immensely charismatic figure, explicitly identified with the god Apollo (*HH* 21), surrounded by the less fortunate who find in him a type of secularised divine hope:

> Only a God with endless resources could permit himself real *largesses*! ... So all those people had clung desperately to what their sun-filled brains insisted was Hugh Monckton Allardyce Smith.
> ... [They] were not out for the goods. ... They desired the companionship, the intimacy, of the God Apollo Fortunatus .... In a crumbling world, if you can stand beside one who possesses bottomless treasures and the person of Helen of Troy you may escape the abyss that awaits the less fortunately accompanied. (*HH* 22, 23)

Hugh Monckton's 'Helen of Troy' is Gloria Sorenson, a married Scandinavian singer with whom he has had a protracted affair. He wishes to take Gloria away from her husband on a long cruise aboard the yacht *Le Secret*, but Gloria seems to prefer her career and husband to Hugh Monckton. Unable to face losing her, and partly as a result of Henry Martin's insensitivity to his appeals for sympathy, the millionaire opts for suicide.

Hugh Monckton's suicide is a success: that of Henry Martin a failure. The result is that almost by accident Henry Martin is substituted for Hugh Monckton, part disguised by a beard grown to cover facial injuries, but unable finally to fool all concerned. The second half of *The Rash Act* and the whole of *Henry For Hugh* are dedicated to Henry Martin's slow and problematic assumption of the role of the wealthy Englishman, and his slow discovery. Pleasurably ensconced in an isolated villa overlooking the Mediterranean, he first has to negotiate the complex *ménage à trois* in which he finds himself accidentally involved. His second problem is adequately to masquerade as Hugh Monckton before an ageing aunt who arrives to look after him. She eventually penetrates his disguise, and also discovers his blood tie to the family. In order to protect the business and the family line she does not give him away, and endorses his deception on her deathbed.

In many ways, these novels of Ford continue to act out an agenda defined by T. S. Eliot in *The Waste Land* and '*Ulysses*, Order and Myth'. The best known passage from the latter will perhaps bear repetition:

> In using the myth, in manipulating a continuous parallel between contemporaneity and antiquity, Mr. Joyce is pursuing a method which others must pursue after him ... It is simply a way of controlling, of ordering, of giving a shape to the immense panorama of futility and anarchy which is contemporary history ... Psychology (such as it is, and whether our reaction to it be comic or serious), ethnology, and *The Golden Bough* have concurred to make possible what was impossible even a few years ago. Instead of narrative method, we may now use the mythical method. It is, I seriously believe, a step toward making the modern world possible for art.[12]

Ford does not, as does Eliot, reject 'narrative method': indeed the two novels are intended perhaps largely as narratologically virtuosic *divertimenti*. But once story is separated from narrative then it becomes apparent that against the background of the futility of the depression years, accompanied by the moral and sexual change of the two preceding decades, Ford has opted for myth as a structuring device.[13] The story is a version of the fable of the prince and the pauper, which is in its turn underpinned by a narrative of regeneration based on the findings popularised in *The Golden Bough*. In this case, and not in strict accordance with Fraser, the Sun God is ritually destroyed and replaced by a successor whose ineffectual decline has been up until this point the reverse of his own continued rise.

It is useful to approach an analysis of these novels with Eliot's own use of myth in *The Waste Land* in mind. There are also important parallels in the novel of the 1920s. At the centre of the narrative is the ineffectual hero who has been unable to fulfil any of what might be seen as the traditional criteria of responsible masculinity, faced by the rise of a New Woman which he cannot comprehend. His marriage has been barren, and the implication is that he is impotent. There is a family resemblance here to *The Sun Also Rises*, with its exploration of the Lost Generation and impotence motif. Towards the close of *Henry For Hugh*,

Henry Martin is revealed to be potent, and the narrative can conclude with him 'getting the girl' and closing the gap of inadequacy which can be seen as the structuring principle of the narrative, a fairy tale conclusion which negates the strictly irreversible fate of Jake Barnes. As in *The Waste Land*, sterility becomes the symbol of the decay of a culture, and in particular of a perceived decay of patriarchy. But the tone is more like that of 'The Love Song of J. Alfred Prufrock'. Tongue-in-cheek and satire abound: these works share a concern with an inadequate masculinity portrayed in an almost constant state of deep anxiety, and deploy the motifs of suicide and cod-Hamlet self-dramatisation to similar effect. Ford's narrative is intended as a salve to the wounded, not a nihilistic celebration of universal sterility: it is a comedy which restores sexual and economic potency through magic. To recognise the ambiguous way in which the writing here constitutes a type of psychological and mythic comedy it is useful to bear in mind Eliot's qualification: psychological analysis is now a part of the modern artistic equipment 'whether our reaction to it be comic or serious'. Richard Cassell has noted that these novels 'sometimes read like parodies of Hemingway, Sherwood Anderson and Ford himself.'[14] The presence of what might more properly be considered pastiche, rather than parody, has contributed to the notable uneasiness of Ford critics in the presence of this book. Perhaps we should allow *The Rash Act* to modify our sense of what is going on in the earlier and better-known works. It is in a peculiar mixture of poker-faced comedy and an often only implicit sombreness that *The Rash Act* and *Henry For Hugh* offer their analysis of the age, registering ultimately a deep anxiety that all of their procedures and the insights that they tentatively offer might be overtaken by a vaster history which they can neither know nor influence, a history implied by the vigorous encroachments of communism and Bonapartism into the protagonist's world (e.g. *RA* 152-3; *HH* 108ff.).

Henry Martin's ill-being is epochal, a function of what has so frequently been interpreted as the epistemological break of the *fin de siècle*: 'it was a mistake to be born in the nineteenth century when the whole of your life was to be passed in the twentieth' (*RA* 28). His irresolution extends perhaps unsurprisingly to his suicide:

> Suicide is an act of despair. Still more it is a confession of ineffectualness. Yet it calls for resolution. ... No, he had never been wanting in resoluteness. ... Then. ...
> It was as if he were not all of one piece. It was perhaps that. Born in the nineteenth and having lived the great part of his life in the twentieth century.
> Resolution was the note of the nineteenth, mental confusion of the twentieth. Perhaps it was that. (*RA* 32)

Or perhaps not. With hesitations, suspensions, ellipses and time-shifts, the narrative traces the irresolute efforts of this decentered male subject to realise itself and its own history.

The protagonist shares with the male protagonists of other novels of the 1910s and 1920s the perception that what are regarded as the normative social relations of the nineteenth century have broken down. Whether these relationships that in retrospect seem so normal were ever in place, in some stable heavenly world of 'Victorian values', we know well enough now to question. Henry Martin, like Theodore Gumbril in Aldous Huxley's *Antic Hay* (1922), has broken from the commercial values of his father in favour of an as yet unrealised artistic ideal. Gumbril faces his situation by engaging in a parody of aggressive commercial marketing activity, designing the Gumbril Patent Small-Clothes – inflatable underwear for sitting on hard seating in public venues. Henry Martin, less effectually and with no comparable sense of humour, has ventured into the world of speculation and been ruined.

Ford's protagonist perceives a breakdown in sexual mores:

> ... It was becoming more and more the fashion for males to regard females as little more than the casual furniture of a man's apartment. You could acquire women as you acquired divans, mattresses or central heating and replace them by other patterns when their attractiveness made them seem a little shop-soiled. ... And women, of course, if their means permitted, could behave exactly the same by men. (*RA* 111)

This complaint is part of a familiar pattern in terms of the fiction of the period. Richard Aldington's *Death of a Hero* (1929) similarly laments 'newfangleness', but its thesis is more decisively misogynistic than that of *The Rash Act*: it seeks to contrast the suffering and austerity of the enlisted male protagonist with the moral dissolution of the women on the home front. The hapless hero, although he subscribes (if somewhat passively) to new ideas about openness in sexual relationships, is portrayed as the naive victim of these ideas and of the fickleness of women. His death in battle takes the form of a suicidal action perpetrated because he can no longer abide the general domestic situation.

In Aldington's work, suffering at the front legitimises the male protagonist's sense of moral superiority to those who have remained at home, especially the women. Although the war is depicted as horrendous and senseless, it serves more as the occasion of Winterbourne's death than as its cause. The war occupies a different structural position in Ford's novels: it is not allowed to give a neat guarantee of moral superiority to either Henry or Hugh. Hugh Monckton is one of the 'Old Contemptibles' – the first British expedition of 1914, termed by the Kaiser a 'contemptibly little army', and in the popular version 'a contemptible little army'. In this early phase open warfare was the rule, it was even possible to deploy mounted troops, and Hugh Monckton was rendered *hors de combat* by a blow to the head from a cavalry sabre, of which he still bears the scar as testimony to a heroism that seems to belong to another age. The Old Contemptibles have a high reputation in France, but Henry Martin is sceptically aware that theirs was the more glamorous and less dangerous part of the war. Hugh Monckton's image is greatly reinforced by this history, however insubstantial the reality that it seems to represent. Once again he is the human god whom it has been necessary to invent:

> From a sword-cut on the Marne to the bed of Gloria Sorenson [...]. An immensely powerful God must be behind that fellow. (*RA* 68-9)

Henry Martin's own role in the war is a matter of bathos. As an American he need have taken no part, but signed up voluntarily. His first experience of conflict is with the authorities: he falls foul of an English N.C.O. due to an ill-defined incident involving alcohol and misplaced heroism, in which 'he had imagined himself defending the poor, bloody Welsh Tommies against the ignorant, brutal oppression of their English superiors' (*RA* 45). When sent abroad, he is given little opportunity for heroism, passing most of the time far behind the lines in charge of a cannery. His participation in the war, mute and inglorious though it has been, has nevertheless aroused the ire of the substantial German-descended section of the population of his native Springfield (*RA* 48). Ford goes to great lengths in *The Rash Act* to give his characters complex, ethnically mixed backgrounds, cross-breeding them forwards and backwards across the Atlantic. Conventional assurances about identity, such as those offered by European aristocracies, are no longer to be had in this mongrelised world. There is an implicit critique of the intensely nationalistic nature of the First World War, and the lesson that, particularly for an American, jingoistic moralism can no longer be the foundation of the heroic self.

In the spirit of other fiction and biography of the period – *Death of a Hero*, or Graves' *Goodbye to All That* (1929) – Henry Martin tries to evaluate the effects of the war on himself. He does not know whether to consider himself the member of a 'Lost Generation', psychologically destroyed by the war, while the narrative keeps the conflict itself always at a certain distance from him:

> He was perhaps one of the *génération perdue* that the French talked of. The Lost Generation. ... They were said to be so disturbed in their equilibrium by the distortions of the late war that they had no sense of the values of life. ... That might of course be the case. But he could not see why he should have been affected. He certainly had not taken the war hard. He had shuffled, really, through it. Not of his own will. (*RA* 48)

Later in the novel the Lost Generation hypothesis is submitted to gentle mockery, in a passage which also indicates a related fear that the new *mores*, and the faddish popular psychology which feeds them, have also destroyed the sacred relationship between mother and son, scarring the latter:

> [His mother] had had the proud idea that rocking babies injured their brains. [...] Henry Martin had *never* been rocked. ... That was the baby-raising craze in those years. ...
> Perhaps that was why he and the boys born about then were now the Lost Generation. They probably needed rocking to form their characters. Well, Providence was about to make up for it. He was going to be. ... What was the old song?
> 'Rocked in the cradle of the deep!' (*RA* 190)[15]

In fact it is the conflict with his father which has precipitated Henry Martin's suicide. This conflict between father and son is again a theme of the literature of the period. Like Kreisler in Wyndham Lewis's *Tarr*, Henry Martin is precipitated towards suicide by a break with his father and the refusal of financial assistance (*RA* 156). The conflict has symbolic and possibly Oedipal connotations. In *Tarr*, a psychological twist has Kreisler – an unfortunate, would-be artist, who is psychologically quite unlike Henry Martin – lose his fiancée to his father. In Henry Martin's case the Oedipal defeat is more ambiguously signalled, but hinges on his Father's surprise arrival in Paris to persuade the son's fiancée not to continue the liaison, which he succeeds in doing (*RA* 63).

The moment in which Henry Martin imagines being 'rocked in the cradle of the deep' is one of a number, scattered throughout the first half of *The Rash Act*, in which he or Hugh Monckton attempts to represent death and thereby give it shape or meaning. At stake in these various attempts to figure death is a concern with the proper: with property or propriety – in fact with the self and its integrity. It is hoped that the self might achieve in death the integrity that it has failed to achieve in life. At least, death will represent an escape from the impotence that each experiences, though Hugh Monckton fears that death might be just another form of the same thing: 'The queer thing about contemplating death is the feeling of complete impotence it gives you' (*RA* 129).

Both Henry and Hugh wish to preserve a propriety in death. Each wishes to be found whole, clean, and well-preserved. Neither wishes to have his body searched, to which end Hugh shoots himself clutching his passport and suicide note in his free hand (*RA* 186, 206). In Henry's self-fantasising, suicide becomes an act of self-creation:

> He had marched there to his end, Nordic hero. Taking his call.
> [...] the curtain had come down on the end of his tragedy. Of that he was both hero and author. (*RA* 188)

Henry's resolution and concentration – his self-possession – are violated both by the shifting recollections which surge up in his mind at times with comic incongruity, and by material factors which seem set to violate the intended perfect image of the suicide victim. As he steers his boat out into the sea in which he intends to kill himself, he notices that the engine is 'not running smoothly. [...] It was as if a mourner had behaved indecorously at his funeral' (*RA* 189).

Ford extracts sly humour from his limited hero's last-minute thoughts on the aesthetics of suicide: cutting his throat or shooting himself would make his corpse 'repulsive'; using the gas oven and dying indoors is disagreeable because he wants to see the sky with his dying eyes. The place of death is equally a source of aesthetic rationalisation:

> He had chosen with great deliberation the place at which he would step off the boat. [...He] had resolved to end it about fifty yards from the left-hand lighthouse – fifty or a hundred.
> A certain fastidiousness may be allowed to one in the choice of the place of one's end! (*RA* 20-1)

A mockery of all attempts to represent self or death in the absence of God lurks beneath such moments. The immediately preceding paragraph declares (presumably in free indirect discourse representing

Henry Martin's own thoughts), that 'He was beyond good and evil' (*RA* 20). The contrast between this ineffectual protagonist and the Nietzschean *übermensch* is stark. But the irony at Henry Martin's expense does not necessarily proceed from a perspective of Nietzschean superiority. We might ourselves choose to say that Henry Martin's evidently existential crisis shows him languishing in post-Christian modes of representation which have failed to exit post-Christian conceptuality, failing that Nietzschean challenge which Nietzsche's own work is often now said not adequately to meet. If we are to project an implied authorial figure here, it is one more akin to the Wyndham Lewis who attacked Nietzsche as a 'vulgarizer', persuading 'all the half-educated [...] student and art-student population of Europe' that they are 'beyond good and evil.'[16] Later in the novel, Henry Martin's stance will become less sub-Nietzschean, moving closer to a vision, such as that at times offered by Lewis, of the indifference of God.[17] This vision unites anti-liberal critique of the notion of a caring deity with the ultimate assurance that reality is ordered by a First Cause beyond or behind its shifting surfaces:

> It was not that he disbelieved in the existence of a Deity. He felt indeed extremely aware of a First Cause. But he believed that the Deity was as indifferent to his existence as he himself was indifferent to that awful presence. [...] It astonished him to find that he felt towards the super-natural economy much as he felt towards the efficient police of a good republic. They had their function, but they were nothing to him and he nothing to them. (*RA* 161)

This passage might be read as the product of the author's own bent toward the Catholic reaction and its Anglo-Saxon equivalents: at any rate it neatly figures the tension between unavoidable recognition of God's absence, and an equally powerful apprehension that there is a conceptual if not personal need for his existence as a principle of order, in particular of political order. In his reference to the police, Henry Martin appears to discover that 'art of being ruled' which the Catholic reaction and its fellow-travellers were to recommend with increasing force through the late 1920s and 1930s. It compares too to the views of Tate and the Agrarians, as expressed in the 'Statement of Principles' of *I'll Take My Stand*: 'Religion is our submission to the general intention of a nature that is fairly inscrutable.'[18]

Hugh Monckton has combatted death by seeking to elide it. What I call here a desire to guarantee the integrity of the self is perceived by Hugh Monckton as a desire to flee the self: his conversation with Henry Martin the night before the suicide touches on the Foreign Legion and the literature of escape (*RA* 87-8). The escape is not from the self, but from world crisis: the Depression. Ford harbours a sense of the relationship between individual psychological malaise and world conditions, which is naturalistic, and has links to the still continuing project to marry materialism and psychoanalysis.[19] Neither Henry nor Hugh is in doubt as to the cause of their suicide: for Henry, 'The Crisis alone was responsible for him taking his own life' (*RA* 186), while Hugh's suicide note specifies that 'He died because the after effects of the late war had become too intolerable for him' (*RA* 206). This may seem like over-simplistic self analysis on the part of the protagonists, but in fact reflects Ford's naturalist ambition for this novel, to tell the story 'in an atmosphere of our own world with the effects and echoes of the Crisis and its machinery creeping in' (*Reader* 267). So convinced is Ford that this is what he is doing that the introduction of Gloria Sorenson is accompanied by the bald judgement (again, seemingly in free indirect discourse and therefore attributable to Henry Martin): 'she seemed to be suffering from the world depression as badly as anyone between there and Wall Street' (*RA* 39). This seems an assertion rather than a demonstration of the connections between individual and epoch, but signals a refusal to fetishise a hypostasised individual psychology. In turn, a tension is established between the fantasy structures of the novel and its naturalistic aspirations.

Hugh Monckton's escape is into the unsustainable fantasy of a self apart. His means of escape is a luxury yacht, *Le Secret*, on which he plans to sail away to the Islands of the Blest in fulfilment of a childhood dream (*RA* 89-92). He turns to suicide when Gloria Sorenson, who is an integral part of this plan, shows herself unwilling to leave her husband to sail with him. The boat has been furnished with a number of unique and valuable items, as if each, in its very particularity should by the association of ownership symbolically underwrite the individual reality if its possessor. If she could be possessed, Gloria Sorenson would be the most outstanding of these possessions: the lesson is that neither she nor the pleasure which she can bestow can be possessed in any way. In Henry Martin's understanding, the collection of valuables can be understood as a counterweight to this white goddess:

> Hugh Monckton had intended to *filer le parfait amour* with that Medusa. For she was like a Medusa: something marmoreal that gazed into the distance. Hugh Monckton had desired to go away for ever on the gorgeous yacht *Le Secret* with that doom-faced phenomenon. He had decided to surround their amours with, as it were, doomed and magic bric-a-brac – a Pheidian Venus, a matchless second folio, a tiara of the Empress Eugénie, a manteo of Cleopatra's day, a harpsichord on which Mozart had played; two pictures of Simone Martini, three of Gaugin's, a Cézanne; an incredibly life-like head of a matron from a Pompeii coffin; Ibsen's first draft of the *Master Builder* – out of compliment no doubt to the lady's Scandinavian origins. [...]
>
> If you sailed to the South Seas with that marble-faced Medusa you would have to have round you objects that braced you up. You could not be alone with that face. (*HH* 71, 72)

The irony of Hugh Monckton's attempts to secure individuality is that he will turn out to be entirely replaceable, as one Smith succeeds another with barely a hiccough – a principle of substitutability which Ford had outlined in *The English Novel*:

> If you no longer allow yourself to take sides with your characters you begin to see that such a thing as a hero does not exist. [...]
> [I]t is far more usual that, when a seemingly indispensable individual disappears for one reason or another from an enterprise, that adventure proceeds with equanimity and very little shock. (*EN* 126)

This is not only a theory of the hero but a theory of personality – or rather its absence – which has potentially drastic consequences for the poetics of the novel.[20] I will in conclusion indicate what some of those consequences are.

What is most striking in this passage is the way in which woman is modelled. In a brief discussion, Timothy Weiss has pointed out that women in this novel are identified with the moon, with whiteness and cold. This is particularly so in the case of Gloria Sorenson. She is identified here as marmoreal and as a Medusa. Elsewhere she is described as a snow-princess: 'She was cold to everybody [...] like the princess with ice-splinters in her heart' (*HH* 37). Eudoxie, who becomes Henry's Gloria, 'forbidden to him as Gloria [Sorenson] Malmström had forbidden herself to Hugh Monckton', supplies 'snow' (cocaine), and is identified by Henry Martin as a 'Siren' or 'Circe' (*RA* 267) and a 'Valkyr' (*HH* 68). Refusing herself to him sexually, knowingly collaborating with him in his deception, Eudoxie refers to their 'Union' as 'a white flame ... a cold oneness' (*HH* 63). Similarly, the English aunt who arrives to look after her nephew is identified with snow and moonlight, although she represents a calming and soothing, rather than a destructive force (*HH* 57). Making connections in particular with Sylvia in *Parade's End*, Weiss claims that these lunar-aspected women are shown as having the power to 'kill or cure.'[21]

It would be premature to identify this modelling of women as the thesis of the novel and thereby of the novelist. It is to a great extent the flawed thesis of the protagonists, an inadequacy of perception of which Henry Martin at least is shown to be intermittently aware:

> He wanted to carry Eudoxie off home and to cast at her feet the jewels of Golconda won by his strong right arm. ... That sort of bilge was undoubtedly working all the time in his undermind! (*HH* 134)

The events of the narrative appear to indicate a gap, possibly unclosable, between the actions and activities of the women and the interpretation of these actions arrived at by the male protagonists. For example, the absence of Gloria, over whom Hugh Monckton commits suicide, might simply be accounted for by her singing commitments in Spain. Gloria is demanding, and this indicates a level of cynicism in her which Henry Martin, now in Hugh's place but immune to her charms, can identify. It was only on Hugh Monckton that she had the effect of a Medusa, not on Henry. Similarly, although Eudoxie is described by Henry Martin as a Circe, events show her to be overwhelmingly undemanding and her actions do not confirm his Circe hypothesis (*RA* 289). She fails to fulfil her allotted role in his libidinal economy.

This gap between (male) interpretation and (female) reality seems to be the operating thesis of these novels. To examine this claim we return to the opening paragraphs of *The Rash Act*. Here, the Mediterranean setting is established in a moment of Imagistic calm and emptiness in which Henry Martin's consciousness is momentarily emptied of its memories and anxieties. In terms of the narrative this is the calm before the storm, before the impressionistic hail begins. The few events which are dealt with in 'real' narrative time are presented through the activity of Henry Martin's mind, as it artfully time-shifts through his thoughts and recollections to create a complex sense of how the present moment is constituted. Without the constant, Bergsonian or Proustian incursion of memory into the present, without that history which the individual is pleased to call its own, a moment of mystical self-evacuation is achieved:[22]

> He was suspended [...] – between nothing and nothing. There was nothing to think of but visible objects. The sea level: blue at the edges. The stone pines bent, red-trunked. The umbrella pines brighter in colour. (*RA* 9)

Later, approaching the 'rash act', Henry Martin is again plunged into a moment of calm presence which contrasts with the anxious flux of his memories and impressions, and imagines Heaven itself to be 'all sunlight and little bright objects' (*RA* 193).

It is Provence which offers this image of the human condition as vision, in all its sheer imagistic visibility. But against the static backdrop, the unvarying real, the subject will project his fantasy:

> If you wanted to attempt suicide with subsequent change of identity where else could you select better to do it than that landscape of stone pines and illusions? [...]
> And indeed in those parts you were safe to find classically featured dark girls beautiful enough to make you cross a room and present them with rings. ... That was the entrance into siren-land, that region. You were safe to find a siren there. As well as a *poule* with a cold. (*RA* 262)

Provence is the home of *'le gaie sçavoir* – the gentle Science' (*Provence* 54), far enough from the Nietzschean variety which has now assumed its name, a conscious indulgence in elaborate, romantic fantasy. Yet Ford's version of romance is perhaps not that far from the Nietzschean vision of the world of the dead God. For it is conscious acceptance of death which underpins the Fordian emphasis on pleasure in his celebration of Provence, where for strong preference he passed much of his adult life. *Provence* repeats the anecdote of the dancing boy of Antibes which is one of the central images of *The Rash Act*:

> [...] I cannot be accused of disliking dancing or of having any contempt for the most lovely as it is the most fugitive of all the Arts. And indeed of all the beautiful and mysterious emotions that go to make up the frame of mind which is Provence the most beautiful, moving and mysterious is that of the Northern Boy of Antibes. The boy danced and gave pleasure, died two thousand years ago and his memorial tablet set into the walls of Antibes [...] sets forth those salient facts of his life and portrays in the lasting stone the little bag in which he used to make his collections.... (*Provence* 49-50)

'SALTAVIT. PLACUIT. MORTUUS EST.' (*RA* 35)

Ford repeatedly referred to Provence as a 'frame of mind' in *Provence* and *Great Trade Route*. This frame of mind, in which transient pleasures are enjoyed in the full knowledge of the transience of pleasure and of the pleasured subject alike, is the antithesis of Hugh Monckton's attempt to monumentalise love and culture aboard *Le Secret*. If there is a secret, it is that pleasure cannot be so conserved. When Hugh fails to master and monumentalise woman – and risks being turned to stone himself by this 'Medusa' – it is left to Henry, acting for Hugh, to continue the 'jolly old beanfeast' of life which Hugh Monckton has not known how to enjoy (*RA* 348).

Henry's subsequent relationships with women are based less on a will to domination than on a perceived need to escape. Yet the very continuation of his existence, his turning back from suicide, is founded on the symbolic overcoming of woman. As he moves toward the moment of killing himself, out at sea on the boat, a sudden storm blows up. His thoughts of suicide are abandoned as survival instincts take over. In this moment he sees the boat as a woman, the 'only friend I have', and with a cry of 'Damn all women!' he sets out to ride the storm (*RA* 199). 'Male and female created he them. ... The boat was a female ...' (*RA* 202).

The metaphor of the boat as female locates a key issue of the book. Henry Martin's self-confidence returns in the triumph of male protectionism when he saves himself and the boat. In this moment, he briefly establishes a relationship with the symbolically feminine which combines harmonic co-operation with protective domination. He has never in his relationship with women managed to achieve this ideal relationship with the feminine, and it is the inability to so arrange his relationship to the symbolic which has led him to despair in the first place.

Henry Martin's relationship with his estranged wife, Alice, has failed for reasons that are not fully apparent to him. Only shortly before his attempted suicide does he realise that Alice may be a lesbian, and that her travelling companion Mrs Percival is probably her lover. Lesbianism had become openly fashionable in the more sexually liberated sections of European and North American societies during the 1920s, as further attested in the literature of the period (whether in the work of Stein or Radclyffe Hall). Lesbianism threatens the symbolic order: Henry Martin, with a lack of awareness that typifies his Prufrockian ineptness in matters sexual, and further blinded by his own interest in Mrs Percival (which she has been careful to cultivate), fails to understand that, in his locality at least, the symbolic order has in effect been short-circuited:

> It was as if he hardly existed for her. ...
> It burst like a shell in his mind that she might be a Lesbian.
> He knew next to nothing about Lesbianism. [...] Sudden excitement filled him. He felt as if he ought to investigate. ... As if he had been wronged. As if he had wrongs that he could declaim about. He had always wanted to have wrongs. ... To be in a position to declaim about them. ... (*RA* 116)

Alice's resort to lesbianism may in its turn be a response to the sterility of their marriage (*RA* 110), or to his own passionlessness: 'the modern man was incapable of passion' (*RA* 101). Lesbianism is the precise opposite of the white goddess myth which Henry Martin sees in his other relationships with women. The male is very much the centre of the white goddess myth, whether he is to be destroyed or cherished by the feminine. Lesbianism simply does not acknowledge male masculinity, however much Henry Martin's self-dramatising instincts attempt still to cast him in the lead role as the tragic hero, declaiming his wrongs. Death is unrepresentable. It is the ultimate impotence, yet in Henry Martin's imagination it becomes the occasion of his own heroism. Lesbianism, with its implied castration-threat, is akin to death in being unrep-resentable: it can be feared, but it points towards an absence of the male subject which cannot properly be represented. This is why Henry Martin cannot know lesbianism, and even imagines it as a mystery akin to death which will remain unknown even after death:

> What, if Alice and Mrs Percival were Lesbians, was Lesbianism? Possibly a desire for a higher union. ... Perhaps his next-world torture would be worrying that he did not know what Lesbianism was. That would be grotesque. ... (*RA* 158)

Ford and Freud are consonant on this issue:

> [D]eath is an abstract concept with a negative content for which no unconscious correlative can be found. [...]
>
> [It is] possible to regard the fear of death [...] as a development of the fear of castration.[23]

That neither death nor castration can be known, in spite of Henry Martin's bathetic attempts to fill this inevitable blank, turns the narrative back to the pleasure principle of wish-fulfilment. Fulfilment is far from immediate, and Henry Martin's self-liberation in the boat episode is short-lived. Henry, now Hugh, finds himself at the centre of a *ménage à trois*, later augmented by Hugh Monckton's aunt and an English maid. These women care for him and, due to his illness, he is dependent on them. Yet they remain as incomprehensible to him in their motives as had Alice (e.g. *HH* 258, 267). The protagonist finds himself helplessly subjected to inscrutable female wills, 'absolutely flat under all those skirts. ... The monstrous regiment of women! Held down! Tied down! Bound on to the tiles of the terrace without a hint of any idea of what they wanted of him ...' (*HH* 250).

Henry Martin, first saved from death, is now saved from symbolic castration and magically restored to potency towards the conclusion of *Henry For Hugh*. Although the English aunt has understood that her real nephew is dead, she accepts him and, in so functioning as a maternal substitute, rectifies one aspect of his relationship to the symbolic (*HH* 296, 299). Henry further learns that his impotence is the temporary effect of medication (*HH* 275). After this he can free himself of his paralysing *ménage à trois* and also from the confines of his assumed role. He flees with Eudoxie, his Gloria, from France, where the police are on his heels, into Italy, where only the presence of Fascist border guards indicates that although his masculinity is restored, there will be no absolute escape from the violences of history.

Like *The Good Soldier* and *Parade's End*, *The Rash Act* is self-consciously modern in its centre-staging of sexual *mores*. Yet the *ménage à trois* with a seemingly impotent man at its centre which dominates the plot following the substitution of Henry for Hugh remains barely comprehensible to the reader, just as it is barely understood by the injured and confused protagonist, who cannot see beyond his own fantasy structures. So while it is the more intriguing and structurally more important feature of the plot, in terms of overall organisation this central mystery takes a decisively second place to the main plot device: the substitution of Henry for Hugh and the potential for discovery. This plot is so artificial as to be metafictional, in the sense that it challenges acceptance at its face value even though it is articulated with so much attempted verisimilitude. It is as if Ford had deliberately set himself a technical challenge. The subject of the double was already a familiar enough one in fiction, and Ford is likely to have had in mind Conrad's 'The Secret Sharer' (1912). But in attempting to use doubling in the absence of any suggestion of the supernatural Ford stretches credulity. Although the use of complex time-shifting at first engages the reader with the characters and other particulars of setting, the 'inverted detective story' elements achieve a dominance in the second volume which renders the narrative at times leaden.

In spite of this structural problem, C. H. Sisson's claim that this is 'contemplation under the disguise of fiction'[24] seems inadequate. The novels have unusual narrative features which can now be categorised. Once *histoire* is disentangled from *récit*, a singular tension becomes apparent between the naturalistic and fantastic elements of the story. Like some low-key and little known encounter between Marx and Freud, at which the two men politely agree to differ, the naturalism of Ford's attempts to render contemporary reality in the spirit of dialectical materialism is in sharp contrast with the vision of social relationships as substantially overdetermined by unconscious fantasy which structures the fairy-tale, wish-fulfilment aspects of the novel. In their turn, both types of narrative are potentially negated by the stasis of death, which cannot be narrated, and the stasis of those imagistic moments of calm which punctuate the narrative, suspend history and mirror the vacancy of death and its abolition of the subject.

The Rash Act and *Henry For Hugh* constitute a comic anatomy of melancholy in which Ford looks beyond the pleasure principle, but allows his limited hero a circumscribed affirmation.

NOTES

1. Introduction to *The Bodley Head Ford Madox Ford. Volume I: The Good Soldier; Selected Memories; Poems*, London, Sydney, Toronto: The Bodley Head, 1962, p. 8.

2. *The Rash Act*, London: Jonathan Cape, 1933. Hereafter referred to in the text as *RA*.

3. Alan Judd, *Ford Madox Ford*, Cambridge, Massachusetts: Harvard University Press, 1991, p. 413.

4. *Henry For Hugh* has never been published in Britain. *The Rash Act* has recently been republished (Manchester: Carcanet, 1982).

5. Letter to Stella Bowen, quoted *P/F* 177.

6. Richard A. Cassell, *Ford Madox Ford: Modern Judgements*, London: Macmillan, 1972, p. 27.

7. See Radcliffe Squires, *Allen Tate: A Literary Biography*, New York: Pegasus, 1971, p. 87, and Max Saunders, *Ford Madox Ford: A Dual Life. Volume II*, Oxford and New York: Oxford University Press, 1996, p. 324.

8. 'The Mediterranean' in Allen Tate, *Poems*, New York: Farrar, Strauss, Giroux, 1977, pp. 66-7.

9. Ford wrote that *The Rash Act* was 'the beginning of a trilogy that is meant to do for the post-war world what the Tietjens tetralogy did for the war' (quoted Judd, p. 413). The name of his protagonist is derived from H. G. Wells's *The Dream: A Novel*, London: Jonathan Cape, 1924. The protagonist of this novel, set in the utopia of a distant future, has dreamed of being one Henry Mortimer Smith in Wells's own England. Two themes are carried over from Wells's novel to Ford's. Wells's (dreamed) protagonist is involved in a complex *ménage à trois*, while the figure who dreams him meditates on the nature of personality: 'What is personality but a memory? If the memory of Harry Mortimer Smith is in my brain, then I am Smith' (p. 314).

DAVID AYERS

10. Judd, p. 418.

11. *P/F* 120 & 194n. Ford refers to Robert McAlmon, *The Village: As It Happened Through a Fifteen Year Period* (1924).

12. In Kermode (ed.), *Selected Prose of T. S. Eliot*, London: Faber & Faber, 1975, pp. 177-8.

13. See the discussion of *The Rash Act* and *Henry For Hugh* in Timothy Weiss, *Fairy Tale and Romance in the Works of Ford Madox Ford*, Lanham, New York, London: University Press of America, 1984, pp. 135-40.

14. Cassell (ed.) *Ford Madox Ford: Modern Judgements*, p. 28. In the same vein Cornelia Cook, in a valuable though somewhat compressed account, sees *The Rash Act* as a 'pastiche modernist novel', and describes it as 'groping in the direction of post-modernist awareness': see Cornelia Cook, 'Going Beyond Modernism' [Review of *The Rash Act*], in Richard A. Cassell (ed.), *Critical Essays on Ford Madox Ford*, Boston, Mass.: G. K. Hall & Co., 1987, pp. 145, 148; originally published in *English* 33, no. 146 (1984), 159-67.

15. Compare Ford's mocking comments on this topic in his review of Pound's *How to Read* in *The New Review* for April 1932: 'The Lost Generation cries out to be provided with faith, ambition and other warm toddies' (quoted *P/F* 106).

16. See Wyndham Lewis, *The Art of Being Ruled*. Illustrated by the Author. Edited with an Afterword and Notes by Reed Way Dasenbrock, Santa Rosa: Black Sparrow Press, 1989, pp. 113-18.

17. See Wyndham Lewis, *The Human Age. Book Two: Monstre Gai. Book Three: Malign Fiesta*, London: Methuen & Co., 1955, on the divine Padishah who rules Heaven and 'has absolutely no interest in men' (p. 168).

18. *I'll Take My Stand: The South and the Agrarian Tradition* By Twelve Southerners (1930). Re-issued with an Introduction by Louis D. Rubin, Jr. and Biographical Essays by Virginia Rock, New York, Harper & Row, 1962, xxiv.

19. A project that began to be realised about this time: see R. Osborne, *Freud and Marx: A Dialectical Study*, London: Victor Gollancz, 1937.

20. On the general erosion of faith in the concept of personality see, *inter alia*, Maud Ellmann, *The Poetics of Impersonality: T. S. Eliot and Ezra Pound*, London: Harvester Press, 1987, and my own *Wyndham Lewis and Western Man*, London: Macmillan, 1992. In a negation of Proustian procedures, Henry Martin finds himself being taken

182

over by memories which are not his own (*HH* 62-4), and discovers that social relations determine the inner life (*HH* 105).

21. Weiss, p. 138.

22. Compare the similar concerns of Wyndham Lewis in *Time and Western Man*, London: Chatto and Windus, 1927, and 'Physics of the Not-Self' (1932), reprinted in *Collected Poems and Plays*, edited by Alan Munton with an Introduction by C. H. Sisson, Manchester: Carcanet, 1979, pp. 195-204.

23. Sigmund Freud, *On Metapsychology: The Theory of Psychoanalysis. Beyond the Pleasure Principle, The Ego and the Id, and Other Works* The Pelican Freud Library Volume 11. Translated by James Strachey: edited by Angela Richards, London: Penguin Books, 1984, p. 400.

24. C. H. Sisson, Introduction to the Carcanet edition of *The Rash Act*, p. 5.

THE CONTRIBUTORS

David Ayers is Senior Lecturer in English and American Literature at the University of Kent at Canterbury. He is the author of *Wyndham Lewis and Western Man* (Macmillan, 1992), *English Literature of the 1920s* (Edinburgh University Press, 1999), *Modernism: A Short Introduction* (Blackwell, 2003) and of articles on various aspects of Modernism.

Pamela Bickley has taught as a Visiting Lecturer at Royal Holloway, University of London, for many years. She also teaches at the Godolphin and Latymer School. She completed a Ph.D. on the subject of Dante Gabriel Rossetti and has published on Yeats and Rossetti. Recent work includes an edition of Mary Shelley's *The Last Man*.

Vincent J. Cheng is the author of *Joyce, Race and Empire* (1995), *Shakespeare and Joyce: A Study of 'Finnegans Wake'* (1984) and *'Le Cid': A Translation in Rhymed Couplets* (1987), as well as many articles on modern literature; and co-editor of *Joyce in Context* (1992) and *Joycean Cultures* (1998). Currently he is completing a book on the topic of 'Authenticity and Identity'. He is the Shirley Sutton Thomas Professor of English at the University of Utah.

Tony Davenport is Emeritus Professor of English at Royal Holloway, University of London. He is the author of a standard work on the *Gawain*-poet and two books on Chaucer, and has also published essays on Ford, Samuel Butler and Virginia Woolf. He is researching Ford's medievalism.

Robert Hampson, Professor of Modern Literature and Head of the Department of English at Royal Holloway, University of London, is the author of *Joseph Conrad: Betrayal and Identity* (Macmillan/St Martin's Press, 1993) and *Cross-Cultural Encounters in Joseph Conrad's Malay Fiction* (Palgrave 2000). He is a former editor of

The Conradian and has edited various works by Conrad and Kipling. He co-edited (with Andrew Gibson) *Conrad and Theory* (Rodopi, 1998), and is currently co-editing (with Max Saunders) a volume of essays on *Ford Madox Ford's Modernity*

Max Saunders, Professor of English at King's College, London, is the author of *Ford Madox Ford: A Dual Life*, 2 volumes (Oxford University Press, 1996) and has edited Ford's *Selected Poems* (Carcanet Press, 1997); *War Prose* (Carcanet, 1999); and (with Richard Stang) *Critical Essays* (Carcanet, 2002).

Paul Skinner has taught at the University of the West of England and the University of Bristol (where he took his Ph.D. on Ford Madox Ford and Ezra Pound). He edited Ford's *No Enemy* (Carcanet Press, 2002), and has published articles on Ford, Pound, and Rudyard Kipling. He lives in Bristol, where he works as a bookseller.

ABBREVIATIONS

The abbreviations listed below have been used in the notes and in citing references to Ford's works within the text. The list is divided into two parts:
  (i) an alphabetical list of works by Ford to which reference is made ;
  (ii) a short list of secondary works to which several references are made.
Additional abbreviations which are used in only one essay are identified at the beginning of the Notes at the end of the essay. A full list of abbreviations to be used in future volumes can be found on the Ford Society web site.

(i) Works by Ford

Call   *A Call* (London: Chatto & Windus, 1910)

AL   *Ancient Lights* (London: Chapman & Hall, 1911); published as *Memories and Impressions* (New York: Harper, 1911) [see *MI*]

B   *The Benefactor* (London: Brown, Langham, 1905)

BSDSG   *Between St Dennis and St George* (London, New York & Toronto: Hodder & Stoughton, 1915)

CA   *The Critical Attitude* (London: Duckworth, 1911)

CP1   *Collected Poems* (London: Max Goschen, 1913)

CP2   *Collected Poems* (New York: Oxford University Press, 1936 [published only in USA])

CW   *Critical Writings of Ford Madox Ford*, ed. Frank
          MacShane (Lincoln: University of Nebraska Press, 1964)

EG   *An English Girl* (London: Methuen, 1907)

EN   *The English Novel* (Philadelphia: J. B. Lippincott, 1929;
          London: Constable, 1930)

FQ   *The Fifth Queen* (London: Alston Rivers, 1906)

GS   *The Good Soldier* (London: John Lane, 1915)

GTR   *Great Trade Route* (New York: Oxford University Press,
          1937; London: Allen & Unwin, 1937)

HH   *Henry for Hugh* (Philadelphia: J. B. Lippincott, 1934
          [published only in USA])

HJ   *Henry James* (London: Martin Secker, 1913)

HM   *The 'Half-Moon'* (London: Eveleigh Nash, 1909 [written
          1907])

Holbein   *Hans Holbein the Younger* (London: Duckworth, 1905;
          New York: Dutton, 1905)

Inheritors *The Inheritors* (with Joseph Conrad) (New York:
          McClure, Phillips, 1901; London: Wm Heinemann, 1901)

IWN   *It Was the Nightingale* (Philadelphia: J. B. Lippincott,
          1933; London: Wm Heinemann, 1934)

JC   *Joseph Conrad* (London: Duckworth, 1924; Boston:
          Little, Brown, 1924)

LWBE   *Ladies Whose Bright Eyes* (London: Constable, 1911; revised version, Philadelphia: J. B. Lippincott, 1935)

LF   *Letters of Ford Madox Ford*, ed. Richard M. Ludwig (Princeton, NJ: Princeton University Press, 1965)

MC   *The Marsden Case* (London: Duckworth, 1923)

MI   *Memories and Impressions* (New York: Harper, 1911) [see *Ancient Lights*]

ML   *The March of Literature* (New York: Dial Press, 1938; London: Allen & Unwin, 1939)

NC   *The Nature of a Crime* (with Joseph Conrad) (London: Duckworth, 1924) [written 1906; published serially 1909 in the *English Review* (pseudonym Baron Ignatz von Aschendrof) and in the *transatlantic review*, 1924]

NE   *No Enemy* (New York: Macaulay, 1929 [written 1919])

NMP   *No More Parades* (London: Duckworth, 1925)

Provence   *Provence* (Philadelphia: J. B. Lippincott, 1935; London: Allen & Unwin, 1938)

PL   *Portraits from Life* (Boston: Houghton Mifflin, 1937) (written for *The American Mercury*). Published in UK as *Mightier than the Sword* (London: Allen & Unwin, 1938)

RA   *The Rash Act* (New York: Ray Long & Richard R. Smith, 1933; London: Jonathan Cape, 1933)

Rossetti   *Rossetti: A Critical Essay on his Art* (London: Duckworth, 1902; New York: E. P. Dutton, 1902)

RY   *Return to Yesterday* (London: Victor Gollancz, 1931)

189

SDN   *Some Do Not . . .* (London: Duckworth, 1924)

SF   *The Shifting of the Fire* (London: T. Fisher Unwin, 1892)

SL   *The Soul of London* (London: Alston Rivers, 1905)

SLL   *The Simple Life Limited* [pseudonym: Daniel Chaucer] (London: John Lane, 1910)

SP   *The Spirit of the People* (London: Alston Rivers, 1907)

TR   *Thus to Revisit* (London: Chapman & Hall, 1921)

WBTA   *When Blood is Their Argument* (New York & London: Hodder & Stoughton, 1915)

YL   *The Young Lovell* (London: Chatto & Windus, 1913)

(ii) Secondary Works

Judd   Alan Judd, *Ford Madox Ford* (London: Collins, 1990)

Mizener Arthur Mizener, *The Saddest Story: A Biography of Ford Madox Ford* (New York: Harper & Row, 1971)

Moser   Thomas C. Moser, *The Life in the Fiction of Ford Madox Ford* (Princeton, NJ: Princeton University Press, 1980)

P/F   Brita Lindberg-Seyersted (ed.), *Pound/Ford: the Story of a Literary Friendship: the Correspondence between Ezra Pound and Ford Madox Ford and Their Writings About Each Other* (London: Faber & Faber, 1982)

Reader   Sondra J. Stang (ed.), *The Ford Madox Ford Reader*, with Foreword by Graham Greene (Manchester: Carcanet, 1986)

Saunders Max Saunders, *Ford Madox Ford: A Dual Life*, Two Volumes (Oxford: Oxford University Press, 1996)

Snitow   Ann Barr Snitow, *Ford Madox Ford and the Voice of Uncertainty* (Baton Rouge & London: Louisiana State University Press, 1984)

THE
FORD
MADOX
FORD
SOCIETY

Ford c. 1915   ©Alfred Cohen, 2000   Registered Charity No. 1084040

This international society was founded in 1997 to promote knowledge of and interest in Ford. Honorary Members include Julian Barnes, A. S. Byatt, Samuel Hynes, Alan Judd, Sir Frank Kermode, Ruth Rendell, Michael Schmidt, John Sutherland, and Gore Vidal. There are currently over one hundred members, from more than ten countries. The Society organizes an active programme of events. Besides regular meetings in Britain, it has held major international conferences in Italy, Germany, and the U.S.A. In 2002 it launched the annual series, International Ford Madox Ford Studies, which is distributed free to members. The first issues include: a reappraisal of Ford's diversity; 'Ford Madox Ford's Modernity'; 'History and Representation in Ford'; and 'Ford and the City';. If you are an admirer, an enthusiast, a reader, a scholar, or a student of anything Fordian, then this Society wants to hear from you, and welcomes your participation in its activities.

The Society aims to organise at least two events each year, and to publish one or two Newsletters. It has also inaugurated a series of Ford Lectures, which have been given by Martin Stannard, Alan Judd, David Crane, Sergio Perosa, and Oliver Soskice.
    To join, please send your name and address (including an e-mail address if possible), and a cheque made payable to 'The Ford Madox Ford Society', to:
    Sara Haslam, Department of Literature, Open University, Walton Hall,
    Milton Keynes, MK7 6AA.
Annual rates:
Pounds sterling: Individuals: £12; Concessions £6; Member Organisations £25
US Dollars: Any category: $25
    For further information, either contact Sara Haslam (Treasurer) at the above address, or Max Saunders (Chairman) on e-mail at: max.saunders@kcl.ac.uk
    The Society's Website is at : **www.rialto.com/fordmadoxford_society**

Henry James and the "Aliens"
In Possession of the American Scene

GERT BUELENS

Amsterdam/New York, NY 2002. IX,164 pp.
(Amsterdam Monographs in American Studies 10)
ISBN: 90-420-1280-3   EUR 35,-/US$ 35.-

Henry James and the "Aliens" intervenes substantially in current debates in James studies, most notably in the key areas of cultural studies, ethnic studies and queer studies. Focusing throughout on questions of identity, and most prominently on how the latter is given shape in the very form of the late style, the book finds that James's response to the ethnic other can be grasped neither as an attempt to police, supervise and master the other, nor as a politics of non-identical surrender to that other. Instead, there is a continuum of identity—akin to the "criminal continuity" that James registers throughout the American scene—in which self and other, native and alien, subject and object adopt alternate roles of control and submission. Both are at times in possession of the American scene and possessed by that scene. Jamesian sexual identity, too, proves to be constantly reconstituted in transitive processes of signification that make it impossible to fix the "I" or the "other" within a fixed framework—be that framework a heterosexual or a homosexual one. The eroticism that strikingly informs the late James can therefore only be captured, if at all, under the rubric of the "queer."

Editions Rodopi B.V.
USA/Canada: One Rockefeller Plaza, Ste. 1420, New York, NY 10020,
Tel. (212) 265-6360,
Call toll-free (U.S. only) 1-800-225-3998, Fax (212) 265-6402
All other countries: Tijnmuiden 7, 1046 AK Amsterdam, The Netherlands.
Tel. ++ 31 (0)20 611 48 21, Fax ++ 31 (0)20 447 29 79
Orders-queries@rodopi.nl   **www.rodopi.nl**

Ezra Pound and Poetic Influence

The Official Proceedings of the 17th International Ezra Pound Conference, held at Castle Brunnenburg, Tirolo di Merano

Edited by Helen M. Dennis

Amsterdam/Atlanta, GA 2001. XII,282 pp.
(Internationale Forschungen zur Allgemeinen und Vergleichenden Literaturwissenschaft 51)
ISBN: 90-420-1523-3   EUR 55,-/US-$ 55.-

This collection of twenty essays investigates a series of different aspects of poetic influence in relation to the major modernist poet, Ezra Pound. The volume commences with five essays on matters to do with translation and poetic influence, which situate Ezra Pound as an important transitional figure between 19th-century and 20th-century translation strategies. The next five essays consider different influences on Pound's poetry, and introduce the reader to new research in a variety of areas, including how specific Chinese cultural artefacts inform his poetry. The following five essays explore Pound's influence on some of his major contemporaries, such as Eugenio Montale and Charles Olson, and also (through the reading he gave her as a girl) on his daughter, Mary de Rachewiltz. The concluding five essays exemplify different approaches to the thorny issue of Pound and politics, and end with two diametrically opposed interpretations of Pound's political / poetic thought. The collection will be of great interest to scholars of Ezra Pound and of modern to postmodern poetry; but it will also serve as a useful and lively introduction to some of the debates within Pound scholarship to students coming to his work for the first time.

Editions Rodopi B.V.
USA/Canada: One Rockefeller Plaza, Ste. 1420, New York, NY 10020, Tel. (212) 265-6360,
Call toll-free (U.S. only) 1-800-225-3998, Fax (212) 265-6402
All other countries: Tijnmuiden 7, 1046 AK Amsterdam, The Netherlands.
Tel. ++ 31 (0)20 611 48 21, Fax ++ 31 (0)20 447 29 79
Orders-queries@rodopi.nl   **www.rodopi.nl**